UNDER THE
GAZE OF GOD

UNDER THE GAZE OF GOD

PERSPECTIVES ON SPIRITUAL DEVELOPMENT

G DAVID WILLIAMS CP

Library of Congress Control Number:		2020922821
ISBN:	Hardcover	978-1-6641-1345-9
	Softcover	978-1-6641-1344-2
	eBook	978-1-6641-1364-0

Print information available on the last page.

Rev. date: 11/27/2020

To order additional copies of this book, contact:
Xlibris
UK TFN: 0800 0148620 (Toll Free inside the UK)
UK Local: 02036 956328 (+44 20 3695 6328 from outside the UK)
www.Xlibrispublishing.co.uk
Orders@Xlibrispublishing.co.uk
815489

CONTENTS

For Rosemary

Introduction

With the drawing of this Love and the voice of this Calling
We shall not cease from exploration
And the end of all our exploring
Will be to arrive where we started
And know the place for the first time.
T.S. Eliot, "Little Gidding"

People who are open to the gaze of God are constantly being created and re-created in the image of Eternal love; they are constantly being shaped into the image of the unseen God (Col. 1:15) by the sublime fashioning of His gaze. "For we are his workmanship created in Christ Jesus." (Eph. 2:10). The gaze of God, according to John of the Cross, is the way God assures us that we are beloved children in whom He is well pleased (Mt. 17:5). At the beginning of the XXXII stanza of the *Spiritual Canticle*, he writes: "When thou didst look on me, Thine eyes imprinted upon me their grace. For this cause didst thou love me greatly. Whereby mine eyes deserved to adore that which they saw in them."[1] In his annotation to the

---

[1] John of the Cross, *Spiritual Canticle*, vol. II. Translated and Edited by E Allison Peers, revised edition, (Westminster, Maryland: The Newman Press, 19) 344.

following stanza, he writes, "It must be known that the look of God works four blessings in the soul -namely, that it cleanses, beautifies, enriches and enlightens it, even as the sun, when it sends forth its rays, dries and warms and beautifies and makes resplendent."[2]

At the beginning of creation: that of the universe and our own personal creation we find God gazing on all that He has made and finding that it is good, that it is very good. It is not as if God is in a self-congratulatory mood, self-satisfied with a job well done; there is no reflective activity in God who is infinite love, because love is always directed at the other rather than the self. This is part of the reason why God is a Trinity of persons, but as they say, that's another story. No, there is no distinction between the gaze of God and His creative activity. By virtue of gazing, there comes into being the object of the divine gaze. And prayer, the food of spiritual growth, is the responseto that gaze and an expression of gratitude for being created.

Doris Silverman, in her essay on attachment, notes that

> infants' emotional responsiveness to the mother, their interest, sustained attention, and visual exploration appear to be optimal in gaze behavior, that is, when

---

[2] *Ibid.* 347.

infants are focused on human faces. Infants' smiling response to caregivers' faces and voice the latter noticed as well in blind children and the caregivers' smiling response to their infants, suggest the genetically programmed adaptive importance of this bidirectional response ... Those prominent, large, round eyes [of the baby] engage mothers in gazing experiences. Extended eye contact is seldom terminated by mother and enhances connection between infant and mother.[3]

Considerations of parallels between human and spiritual development lead to the assumption that we are genetically programmed from conception and birth towards a relationship with God. The relationship we enjoy with God as adults mirrors the one we had with our mothers when we were babies, a relationship built on the foundational experience of the first feed. The archaic experience of the first feed, because of its novelty, intensity, and the satisfaction it provided, became internalised and, together with the successive experiences of being fed, resides in unconscious memory traces throughout life. Equally important for human and spiritual development is the fact that the first feed set the foundation for all subsequent experiences of intimacy, closeness, and pleasure.

_____

[3] D. Silverman, "Attachment Research: An Approach to a Developmental Relational Perspective" in Skolnick, ed., *Relational Perspectives in Psychoanalysis,* (Warshaw, SC: Hillsdale, NJ: The Analytic Press, 1992) 201-202.

Infants are programmed to elicit responses of care. Those infant coos, gurgles, and giggles which elicited a desired response in our natural mothers (if we were fortunate enough to have mothers who were responsive to our overtures) also elicited, and continue to elicit, a favourable response in our mothering God. As communication between mother and infant is nonverbal, for the very word *infant* means *incapable of speech*, so, too, contemplative prayer possesses the same nonverbal quality, a quality we describe as ineffable because no words are sufficient to describe the experience. Just as the infant is incapable of articulating and verbalising thoughts and feelings in intelligible language, so too the experience of direct relationship with God is incapable of being verbalised, except perhaps in metaphor, music, and poetry.

The idea of a mothering God holds a significant place in the way many authors interpreted the way God breaks into the life of the world: There is a golden thread running through the course of sacred history reflecting this aspect of God, which may be obscured by the more conventional understanding of God as Father. The Psalmist describes his relationship with God which he likens it to that of a child at his or her mother's breast: "I do not occupy myself with things too great and too marvellous for me. But I have calmed and quieted my soul, like a child quieted at its mother's breast; like a child that is quieted is my soul" (Ps. 131:1-2).

From a different perspective on the mothering of God, we find that in his thirteenth century hymn *Adoro te devote,* Thomas Aquinas used the image of a pelican to signify how Jesus sheds his blood for us and feeds us. From mediaeval times, the pelican has replaced the symbol of the lamb and has been used as a symbol both of the Lord's Passion and of the Eucharist. The pelican represents Eucharist because legend has it that, in times of famine, the mother bird pecks her own breast to feed her chicks with her blood. And so it is that the power of this primitive myth lies in its ability to evoke an image of the self-sacrificing motherhood of God.

Henry Suso, the German mediaeval mystic, born c. 1300, used the mother-child image to describe his own experience of prayer:

> Thus it grew into a habit with him, [Suso himself] whenever he heard songs of praise, or the sweet music or stringed instruments, or lays, or discourse about earthly love, immediately to turn his heart and mind inwards, and *gaze abstractedly upon his loveliest Love*, whence

all love flows.... And thus it fared with him as with a sucking child which lies encircled by its mother's arms upon her breast. (italics added)[4]

Some one hundred years later, in England, Dame Julian of Norwich writes:

But now it behoveth me to say a little more of this forthspreading, as I understand it in the meaning of our Lord: how that we are brought again by the Motherhood of mercy and grace into the kindly state, wherein we are made, by the Motherhood of kind love; which kind love never leaveth us.[5]

The reason why I choose such a model of spiritual development is because grace is built on nature, and in order to have a clearer understanding of how spiritual development occurs, it is helpful to have a clearer understanding of how nature, at least in its human expression, works. What better way is there to understand how human nature works than by going back to human life in its infancy? After all, spiritual commentators take pains to state that, like all journeys, spiritual life has a beginning, a middle and an end. If we are to start at the beginning, then the logical place to start is with

---

[4] In E. Underhill, *Mystics of the Church* (Cambridge: James Clarke, 1925) 143.
[5] Julian of Norwich, *The Revelations of Divine Love*, Translated by James Walsh, (Wheathampstead: Anthony Clarke, 1980) 163.

the earliest experiences of human being, that is, in infancy. T.S Eliot sets the trajectory for our journey in his poem *East Coker,* "In my beginning is my end,"[6] and he continues with the theme in his reflection that "home is where one starts from."[7]

But there is another, more profound, reason for focusing on the mother-infant dyad: The main insight of the book is that the movement into union with God is circular rather than linear; it is not exclusively a movement into something new, something that has not previously occurred, but is also, and more importantly, a movement towards recapturing something which has already existed, namely, that relationship we enjoyed, albeit pre-consciously, at our mothers' breast when God looked upon us and saw that we were very good. Unlike our mothers, however, God does not gaze on us from without, at a distance, but from the deepest recesses of our being. Further, as we have all been babies, we carry vestiges of preconscious memories of a multitude of experiences: of being held, of being cuddled, of being sung to, of being soothed, and of being fed, thousands

---

6   T.S. Eliot, *Four Quartets* revised edition (East Coker: Faber and Faber, 1979) 21.
7   *Ibid.* 27.

of daily experiences which we bring to our encounter with the mothering of God.

Spiritual Development understood a return to the beginning is far from new. In Sermon 53, Meister Eckhart writes

> The Father speaks the Son always, in unity, and pours out in him all created things. They are called to return into whence they have flowed out. All their life and their being is a calling and a hastening back to him from whom they have issued[8]

The pouring out in Jesus of all created things and the call to return are reminiscent of the way Dame Julian describes the process in the passage cited earlier: Where Meister Eckhart writes of a "pouring out," Julian writes of a "forthspreading," a beautiful image of birthing; where Eckhart writes of the call to return to the place from whence all created things came, Julian writes of how "we are brought again by the Motherhood of mercy and grace into the kindly state, wherein we are made, by the Motherhood of kind love."[9] These are wonderful images, indeed, of creation, birth, mothering, and return.

---

[8] Meister Eckhartt, The Essential Sermons, Commentaries, Treatises, and Defence, *The Classics of Western Spirituality* (London: SPCK, 1981) 205.

[9] Julian of Norwich, *The Revelations of Divine Love*, trans James Walsh (Wheathampstead: Anthony Clarke, 1980) 163.

Johannes Tauler, a contemporary of Henry Suso, who was a disciple of Meister Eckhart and is regarded as one of the more important of the Rhineland Mystics, stresses that it is in our beginnings where we encounter God. In his book *The Inner Way,* he writes that we shall never find God unless we

> lift up our souls in the Beginning. Therefore we must pierce through all things that are beneath God and are not God, and the Beginning (from which we have our being) seek earnestly again; for therein alone is our dwelling and the future resting place of our eternal bliss.[10]

From the perspective of psychoanalysis, we enter into the realm of mystical experience through a perpetual return to the place where we started, at the mother's breast. In her lecture *Psychoanalysis and Art,* Marion Milner reflects on the work of Anton Erenzweig, of whom she writes that

> he also discusses that class of people who have forgone the attempt to relate their visions to surface perception -the mystics.... Ehrenzweig goes on to point out how Freud also talked about the mystical state, a state which he described as being one with the universe. Freud called it oceanic ... [and] he explained it as a regression to the early infantile state of consciousness, to the state when the child's ego is not yet differentiated from the surrounding world. Hence, says Ehrenzweig, Freud is claiming that the feeling of union is no mere illusion, but

---

[10] J. Tauler, *The Inner Way*, trans. Arthur Wollaston Hutton, (London: Methuen and Co. 1901).

the correct description of a memory of an infantile state
otherwise inaccessible to direct introspection.[11]

This point illustrates why I suggest that spiritual
development engages us in a movement which is cyclical and
recurring. It is the journey from time into eternity, a journey
which allows God to rectify the mistakes of the past and
redeem our tomorrows. T. S. Eliot begins his poem *Burnt
Norton* with the lines

> Time present
> and time past
> Are both perhaps present in time future,
> And time future contained in time past.
> If all time is eternally present
> All time is irredeemable.[12]

If, as Eliot conjectures, time lies eternally in the present
moment, then it is irredeemable. The point of taking the
view that spiritual growth involves allowing the God of our
tomorrows to bring us out of the present moment, in fact, to
bring us out of the temporal dimension altogether, is because
present time is incapable of change. Encounter with God
in prayer draws us into the realm of the eternal because He

---

[11] M. Milner, *The Suppressed Madness of Sane Men* (London New York: Routledge, 1987) 195, 96.

[12] T.S. Eliot, "Burnt Norton," *Four Quartets,* Revised Edition, (London: Faber & Faber, 1979) 13.

dwells outside time, and when we allow the Lord into our hearts, then that encounter must lie outside time. What this accomplishes, as we come before God in prayer, is that our past, present, and future lie open to His gaze. What happens in a linear approach to spiritual development is that we leave the past behind and move resolutely into our future. If such be the case, then times past cannot be changed, and mistakes cannot be rectified because they are locked in times past. By contrast, what I believe happens when we come before God in prayer is that all our yesterdays and all our tomorrows come before His loving gaze. As a consequence, God is able to touch our yesterdays with His healing gaze. This means that the failings of the past, the regrets we have over mistakes made, regrets over words we wish we hadn't spoken, are healed by the touch of the Divine Physician. This is why it is essential to understand spiritual growth and development as transcending time and allowing us to return, in Eliot's words, to the place where we started and discover the place for the first time. We discover the place for the first time because we see a place renewed, cleaned, healed, and enlightened by the gaze of God, a living gaze which has mended the mistakes of the past and healed the wounds of time.

The movement of return is towards a time and place when our encounter with God was established. We share the same history as Jeremiah and are bathed in a love that preceded our birth: "Before I formed you in the womb I knew you, and before you were born I consecrated you" (Jer. 1:4). And in Psalm 139 we read:

> For thou didst form my inward parts, thou didst knit me
> together in my mother's womb ...
> Thou knowest me right well, my frame was not hidden from thee
> when I was being made in secret,
> intricately wrought in the depths of the earth.
> for thou didst form my inward parts, thou didst knit me
> together in my mother's womb ...
> Thou knowest me right well, my frame was not hidden from thee
> when I was being made in secret,
> intricately wrought in the depths of the earth.
> *Thy eyes beheld my unformed substance.*
> (Ps. 139, 13- 16, italics added).

To enter deeply into prayer is to return to an infant (but not infantile) relationship with the mother, resting on her breast, lost in reverie, open to the gaze of God. It is not infantile because we bring all the faculties of memory, understanding, and will to the enterprise; it is an infant relationship because there is no place for words: infants, as noted above, are incapable of speech. Mystical experience, by definition, is ineffable, incapable of being articulated in words, and as such, remains silent before the gaze of God.

Why is it so important to adopt a cyclical approach to spiritual development? This is a book about spiritual development which is understood to mirror and replicate our emotional, psychological, cognitive and social development. The main thrust of this book is that the spiritual journey runs parallel to and intertwines with our normal human journey through life and embraces all facets of human nature: emotional, psychological and social. The contours of our spiritual journey are shaped by our genetic makeup and environmental influences. By this, I mean that our spiritual nature, just like our human nature, does not change; it develops and matures but remains basically the same.

Consider James and John whom Jesus called "sons of thunder" (Mk. 3:17), the ones who wanted to call down fire and brimstone upon the heads of the inhospitable Samaritan villagers (Lk. 9:54). James and his brother were irascible and short-tempered, probably until the day they died. Peter apparently lacked moral fibre and the courage of his convictions throughout his life; even after denying his Lord, he still bowed before the pressure of public opinion. Paul writes, "But when Cephas came to Antioch I opposed him to his face, because he stood condemned. For before certain men came from James, he ate with the Gentiles; but when they came he drew back and separated himself, fearing the circumcision party. And with him the rest of the Jews acted insincerely." (Gal. 2:11-13a). We do not change personality or our basic temperament (character is another matter); we do, however, develop and grow, hopefully becoming more aware of and sensitive to our own frailty and more compassionate towards the frailty of others.

Human development is described as "a progressive series of changes that occur in a predictable pattern as a result of an interaction between biological and environmental factors."[13] Spiritual development possesses all the qualities of human development but adds the crucial dimension of direct interaction with God, in which the Lord is understood to provide, if I may put it a little crudely, the environmental factor

---

[13] N. J. Salkind, *Theories of Human Development* (New York: John Wiley and Sons, 1985) 2.

and the human psyche, which cannot be separated from the soma, constitutes the genetic factor. I understand God to be environmental in the same way that Paul describes Him in his sermon on the Areopagus: "Yet he is not far from each one of us, for 'In him we live and move and have our being'" (Acts 17:27-28). God is the air which we breathe the ocean in which we swim.

Because the aim of this book is towards growth and development, its orientation is towards original goodness rather than towards original sin. Donald Winnicott, a paediatrician and psychoanalyst, in his paper *Morals and Education* writes,

> Religions have made much of original sin, but have not all come round
> to the idea of original goodness, that which by being gathered together
> in the idea of God is at the same time separated off from the
> individuals who collectively create and re-create this God concept …
> man continues to create and re-create God as a place
> to put that which is good in himself, and which he might
> spoil if he kept it in himself along with all the hate
> and destructiveness which is also found there.[14]

Teilhard de Chardin in *Le Milieu Divin* expresses it somewhat differently but with equal force: "The soul with which we are dealing is assumed to have already turned

---

[14] D.W. Winnicott, "Morals and Education." In The *Maturational Processes and the Facilitating Environment.* (Madison, CT: International Universities Press, 1965) 94.

away from the path of error."[15] Drawing on the insights of developmental psychology, I propose a way of understanding prayer and spiritual development which differs from classical approaches to prayer and mysticism. Often we hear that the journey is fraught with difficulty; that it is a journey based on detachment, self denial and discipline. Received wisdom demands that progress in prayer is linear; depends on faithfulness to the discipline of prayer; engages in a successive movement of detachment from material possessions; and, not to put too fine a point on it, not much fun. Not that these prerequisites for a healthy prayer life are unimportant; they are very important, but they must be seen and interpreted in the light shed by the gentle gaze of God.

The perspectives on spiritual development adopted in this book are different from those we find in traditional spiritual writings. I understand spiritual development as a dynamic interaction between God and human becoming (I use the phrase "human becoming" rather than "human being" because we are always evolving; we are always a work in progress and

---

[15] P.Teilhard de Chardin, (*Le Milieu Divin*. New York: Collins, Fontana Books, 1978) 44.

always shall be, even into eternity). Spiritual development, therefore, is viewed as dynamic not static; collegial and fluid not hierarchical; cyclical not linear; personal not institutional; a movement in phases not a movement in stages; feminine rather than masculine; self-accepting not self-rejecting: all movements brought harmoniously together under the wondrous gaze of God.

I reiterate that the image central to the theme of this book is that of the God-Mother who gazes fondly on her baby and the other equally important image is that of the gleam in the eye of God which we become in response to that gaze. The human self is a reflective entity; so too is the spiritual self, coming to be as a reflection of what God sees. In terms of human development, we gain a sense of self through a process by which we internalise and reflect the myriad ways that others, particularly our primary caregivers, influence us with their values and shape us with their assumptions and prejudices. Our spiritual identity, I repeat, is formed in a way which reflects the manner in which our emotional, psychological, and social identity is formed. In other words, we become that by which we are addressed by God. Our spiritual identity is formed by the multiple ways we reflect the gaze of God.

On the subject of identity formation, the sociologists Berger and Luckmann write:

> The child identifies with the significant others in a variety of emotional ways. Whatever they may be, internalisation occurs only as identification occurs. The child takes on the significant others' roles and attitudes, that is, internalises them and makes them his own. And by this identification with significant others the child becomes capable of identifying himself, of acquiring a subjectively coherent and plausible identity. In other words, the self is a reflective entity, reflecting the attitudes first taken by significant others towards it; the individual becomes what he is addressed as by his significant others. This is not a one-sided mechanistic process. It entails a dialectic. [16]

Spiritual growth occurs as a result of a dialectic process, the fruit of a relationship between God and the soul. In addition to the mothering role of God, there is also the part played by the child. In chapter 18 of his Gospel, Matthew calls us to become as little children: "At that time the disciples came to Jesus, saying, 'Who is the greatest in the kingdom of heaven?' And calling to him a child, he put him in the midst of them, and said, 'Truly, I say to you, unless you turn and

---

[16] P. L. Berger & T. Luckmann, *The Social Construction of Reality* (Harmondsworth: Penguin Books, 1971) 151-52.

become like children, you will never enter the kingdom of heaven" (Mt. 18:13). Entry into the kingdom involves two movements: first, an act of perpetual turning, or conversion and secondly, a recapturing of that relationship with God which we enjoyed as little children. This by no means implies infantilising ourselves, but it does mean embracing a paradox which at times, like most Gospel paradoxes, can be extremely uncomfortable. The nature of this particular paradox is that we become more liberated the more we surrender to its power; that is, by living dependently on God, we become independent and autonomous. Freedom, I maintain, is the goal of all spiritual growth. This is in line with what Paul writes in his second letter to the Corinthians: "Now the Lord is the Spirit and where the Spirit of the Lord is, there is freedom" (2 Cor. 3:17). With the Spirit of God dwelling in the depths of our being, we experience both the call and the impetus towards freedom.

The return to the child-parent relationship is one of constant movement. Each time we enter the state of prayer, we bring with us all that we have gained previously from being touched by God; each time we enter the state of prayer, we enter an infinite spiral at a deeper immersion point, and by doing so, our spirit becomes more expansive. The wider the spirit expands, the greater its capacity to receive more of the divine presence. Teresa of Avila puts it somewhat differently when she says that two souls may equally be filled to capacity with grace, but whereas one soul is the size of a thimble, another soul may be the size of a bucket. Prayer expands the spirit, and because we are destined to live without end, our capacity for growth into the mystery of the Divine is equally infinite.

The movement of return to the place where we started is one Julian captures in the passage quoted above. She writes of how "we are brought again by the Motherhood of mercy and grace into the kindly state, wherein we are made, by the Motherhood of kind love." Notice the words she uses: a) "*we are brought again,*" meaning that we revisit a state of being we had previously enjoyed; b) "*into the kindly state wherein we are made*", meaning that we are being created, that we are becoming, that we are receptive to the work of God and, hence, not in the driving seat, not in control of the process, but are brought into being by the force of a love beyond all telling and, further, that being drawn into the kindly state wherein we are made is a perpetual process of re-creation which occurs and re-occurs again and again, drawing us deeper and deeper into the spiral of divine love.

This approach to prayer is markedly different from those traditionally presented. The spiritual journey, as presented historically, describes a movement (or several movements) towards interiority and is traditionally conceived as having the following characteristics: it is (1) hierarchical; (2) institutional; (3) linear; (4) static; (5) formulated as a stage theory; (6) masculine; and (7) contingent upon self-abasement and self-denial.

Let us briefly take a look at each of these characteristics in turn:

Hierarchical: Pseudo-Dionysius, writing at the beginning of the sixth century,[17] coined the word hierarchy to describe the relationship between the hierarch (bishop) and those subordinate to him. For him, all reality is hierarchical and composed of triads. Pseudo-Dionysius adopted a structure based on Neo Platonic philosophy, which we won't dwell on here. However, for Pseudo-Dionysius, the world of angels and of humans is triadic, that is, composed of three orders

---

[17] P. Rorem, *Pseudo-Dionysius: The Complete Works,* (New York, Paulist Press, 1987) 1.

The holy sacraments [of Holy Orders] bring about purification, illumination, and perfection. The deacons form the order which purifies. The priests constitute the order which gives illumination. And the hierarchs [bishops], living in conformity with God, make up the order which perfects.[18]

These three paths of purification, illumination and union have become enshrined in subsequent ways of understanding spiritual development. In Dionysius's hierarchical structure there is little consideration given to those living in the lay state and he somewhat quaintly assumes that the higher the clerical office, the more intimate is the union with God (yet, alas, history has frequently proved him wrong).

Let me pose a question to demonstrate how a hierarchical structure is largely irrelevant to spiritual development: We are all familiar with Francis of Assisi but who was the parish priest of Assisi at the time? No? Let's ascend the hierarchical ladder. Who was the bishop of his diocese? No? Then who was the pope at the time? All good men, but their names are long forgotten with the possible exception of Pope Innocent III, perhaps because they fail to capture the poetry and magic

---

18 P.Rorem, "The Uplifting Spirituality of Pseudo-Dionysius" in McGinn et al., *Christian Spirituality, Origins to the Twelfth Century*, (New York: Crossroad, 1985).

in the way Francis did. When we come right down to it, the spiritual journey is a journey into poetry and magic. If not, it's not worth the effort.

A hierarchy (ιεραρχία) has come to mean a structure in which people, objects and categories are placed in relationship to one another spatially, with one above the other in an ascending order of relative importance and the structure is pyramidal in shape. Paul, in the twelfth chapter of his first letter to the Corinthians sets the tone for prioritising spiritual gifts in a hierarchical order. He arranges the gifts in order of importance: the highest gift for him, is apostleship and this stands to reason if we consider that Paul is an apostle and, without much modesty, claims the highest gift for himself. As a logical construct it has the advantage of having a place for everything and everything in its place.

Those of a certain age may remember a TV sketch on television in 1966 in which John Cleese represents the upper class, Ronnie Barker the middle class and Ronnie Corbett the working class. The sketch satirises the structure of the British class system. A system of hierarchy, when applied to people, offers an ordered social structure but the social structure it offers labels individuals and these labels create stereotypes which can stifle the spirit. The concept of hierarchy, at least in its original sense, is static, one which restricts social mobility and when applied to spiritual development can stunt that growth which, of its very nature, demands fluidity and flexibility. In contrast to a hierarchical model, I propose one which is collegial, one based on the conviction that we are all equally children of God and that we are the body of Christ, each having a unique role to play in the building up of the body.

Institutional: An institution is a structure having a slow rate of change and, as such, is ill-equipped to foster spiritual development and growth. Ana Maria Rizzuto, in her essay *Religious Development: A Psychoanalytic Point of View,* contrasts religion as institution with personal religion. She writes,

> Organized religions are cultural institutions that offer beliefs, rituals, and communal means of dealing with the tensions of life. They provide the individual with accepted ways of tolerating and integrating the polarities of life by offering symbolic and semiotic systems capable of mediating between personal life, transcendent realities, and the culture of the historic moment. Personal religion is the private and idiosyncratic set of beliefs, convictions, and rituals of a particular individual that form the background for his

or her attribution of religious meaning to [19]events and experiences. The official God of organized religions may be very different from the God of experienced subjective reality, a fact often and easily overlooked.[19]

Most of us gain our concept of God from organised religion; we are taught to pray using formal words and formal gestures. I remember vividly my first introduction to prayer. I was made to kneel on a cold floor while my mother sat on my bed; made to join my hands in a certain way; made to bow my head and made to recite words which I found alien and meaningless. It was a bit like being made to eat spinach: you do it because it is good for you. My introduction to prayer was an introduction to Mr Official God. This is the God who officiates over formal gatherings such as church services and other public acts of worship. This is the God who demands that we do certain things and avoid doing others, and so on. There are many who remain locked into an understanding of God which is deeply unsatisfying because it reflects an earlier stage of development. The God who is worshipped is is a God who involves us in activities: saying prayers, going to church, contributing to the support of those less fortunate. it can be

[19] 9 A.M.Rizzuto, "Religious Development: A Psychoanalytic Point of View," *New Directions for Child Development*, no, 52, Jossey-Bass Inc. Summer 1992.

deeply unsatisfying because the image of God is like a pair of shoes which are too small for the feet: they are tight and pinch the toes. Instead of abandoning the idea of a toe-pinching God, people are too apprehensive to launch out into the deep and trust the God Who calls them to kick off their shoes, wiggle their toes, and move into intimacy and freedom.

Spiritual development, by contrast, is private, idiosyncratic and personal. It consists not in what we say or do but what is done to us. Under the gaze of God, we remain still; we remain passive. Nor is spiritual development necessarily aligned to organised religion. The life and work of Vincent Van Gogh illustrates this point. His father was a minister, and Vincent originally wished to follow in his father's footsteps. In 1876, he taught Bible classes in Isleworth, Middlesex, and on his return to the Netherlands he studied for the ministry but failed his exams. He later rejected the church and claimed in one of his letters, that the best way to know God is to love many things: a friend, a wife, something, whatever you like and you will be on the way to knowing more about Him. Although he did not paint overtly religious subjects, there is an abiding sense of the spiritual in many of his paintings, particularly his wheat fields which have a biblical symbolism. Separating himself from organised religion, Van Gogh developed an inner life of extraordinary depth and beauty, manifested in his art.

Linear: A linear understanding of spiritual development mirrors an understanding of a socio-psychological stage theory of human development. A linear interpretation of spiritual development favours a line of development that, in one of its expressions, ascends from bottom to top, such as that described by Augustine in his *Confessions*: "Step by step was I led upwards, from bodies to the soul."[20] A similar approach is followed by many of the great spiritual authors: by Guigo II in his *Ladder of Monks*; Walter Hilton in his *Scale of Perfection,* and by John of the Cross in his *Ascent of Mount Carmel.* Other writers, such as Teresa of Avila, adopt a different linear model, one which proceeds horizontally rather than vertically, from the outside to the inside. St Teresa, reportedly, had a revelation from God of a crystal globe in the shape of a castle containing seven mansions and wrote *The Interior Castle* as her interpretation of that vision; she describes the journey of

---

[20] Augustine of Hippo, *Confessions*, VII, xvii, 23.

faith as one passing through seven stages ending with union with God in spiritual marriage.

It must be said, however, that when both Teresa and John present spiritual development as a linear progress, either up Mount Carmel (in John's case) or an inward journey from outside to inside, as does Teresa, both are acutely aware that the journey folds back on itself, that the movement into union with the Divine is fluid, and the energy flows in both directions. Teresa reminds us that

> There is no soul so great a giant on this road but has frequent need to turn back, and be again an infant at the breast; and this must never be forgotten. I shall repeat it, perhaps many times, because of its great importance -for among all the states of prayer, however high they may be, there is not one in which it is not often necessary to go back to the beginning.[21]

Also, when she compares the soul to a garden, she writes of four ways of watering the garden. Gerald May writes:

> As was the custom in her time, Teresa's description of these four degrees sounds like a direct progression from meditation through contemplation to the prayer of union. This makes it all too easy to assume a stepwise advancement from one stage to the next. As with John's stages of the night, though, Teresa's degrees of prayer are

---

[21] Teresa of Avila, *The Life of St Teresa of Jesus*, Translated by David Lewis, fifth edition (Thomas Baker, 1932) 102.

not to be understood as occurring in a strictly linear way.
They continually overlap and recur in cycles.[22]

However, the overriding impression created by writers on the journey into union with God is one of a progression through successive stages of development which they present in terms of a linear development. These classical formulations of the spiritual journey have stood the test of time, and I must admit to a certain degree of hesitancy in suggesting another way of looking at the development of our relationship with God. Putting these doubts and fears into the hands of God, let us proceed.

Static: In the year 1543, Copernicus came to the startling discovery that the sun, not the earth, is the centre of the solar system, yet it took some two hundred years before his discovery was universally accepted. In the sixteenth century everyone knew that the earth was the centre of the universe. In spite of the voyages of Columbus, Magellan and da Gama, everyone knew that the earth is flat. The earth is static and everything else revolves around it. The sun rises; the sun sets;

---

[22] G. May, *The Dark Night of the Soul* (Harper Collins, 2009) 115.

end of discussion. This cosmic view coloured the way spiritual development was interpreted. Every treatise on prayer, every spiritual classic until the eighteenth century was written with the common understanding the earth was motionless and this informed a way of interpreting the spiritual life.

By contrast, I would advocate a different approach, one which favours a dynamic rather than static interpretation, more in accord with cosmic reality. I propose that we think of spiritual development in terms of verbs rather than nouns, that we think of rising rather than resurrection; of ascending rather than ascension; of saving rather than salvation, and so on. The dynamism of spiritual growth is to be understood not only in verbal form but also in the present tense of the verb. Jesus is rising and ascending into the bosom of His Father here and now and we are drawn up by the attraction of that movement, one which extends and continues into eternity.

Formulated as a stage theory of development: Classical theories of spiritual development lean heavily on a stage approach, that is, a progression through a series of discrete stages culminating in union with God. Formulating spiritual development as a stage theory implies an abruptness of change from one stage to the next which suggests a discontinuity between stages. Entering one stage implies the successful completion of a prior stage. One cannot achieve stage three without first having achieved the first two stages. A classical example of this way of thinking is to be found in *The Ladder of Monks*: Guigo II writes, "Four stages in spiritual exercise came into my mind: reading, prayer, meditation, and contemplation. These make a ladder for monks by which they are lifted up from earth to heaven."[23] One ascends the ladder one rung at a time, from the lowest to the highest, and the underlying assumption is that the movement is progressive, in that there is no going back to a lower level.

The reason for an alternative approach rests again on the assumption that grace is built on nature which is in perpetual motion. This movement is both cyclical and expansive. We live on a planet which is constantly revolving on its axis at just over 1,000 miles an hour at the equator; like it or not, we are spinning around the sun in an elliptical orbit at 18.5 miles

---

[23] Guigo II, *The Ladder of Monks and Twelve Meditations*, Translated by Edmund College, O.S.A. and James Walsh, S.J. (Mowbray, 1978) 81-82.

per second; and the planet on which we live wobbles back and forth on its axis roughly 23° degrees off centre in the course of a year. This means that one hemisphere of the earth points away from the sun at one side of the orbit, and six months later, this pole will point towards the sun (the reason for our changing seasons).

This is not the only consideration to be borne in mind; we also have to contend with the fact that the whole universe is expanding. If the earth is in constant movement, and the nature of that movement is wobbly and expanding into infinity, then it may be inferred that our journey, both human and divine is wobbly and in constant motion, and that motion is essentially expansive.

Adopting an alternative approach to that of stage theory, we shall interpret spiritual growth as a phase approach. By this, I mean that spiritual growth may be viewed, as mentioned earlier, as cyclical rather than linear, replicating the rhythms of the seasons, the ebb and flow of tides, the waxing and waning of the moon. Each time we come to prayer, we come in a variety of different moods; we come affected by all the events which have most recently touched our lives; we come in seasons of dryness and in seasons of contentment; we are touched by world events; we come in fullness and emptiness; in joy and in grief. We never come to prayer in exactly the same way we did on the previous occasion when we prayed. Our spiritual growth is seasonal which accounts for the experience that so many people recount with disappointment and discouragement when they say things like, "Why is it that I've spent all these years in prayer and yet sometimes it feels like I'm back where I started?" One of the reasons for this, I suggest, is because spiritual development demands that we are "with the drawing of this Love and the voice of this Calling," brought back to the place where we started, a place which seems so familiar, in order to discover the place for the first time. Whereas the earth orbits the sun and returns to the place where it started, we return to the place where we started but at a deeper, more profound level as we move into the infinite love which enfolds us. "For thus said the Lord God, the Holy One of Israel, 'In returning and rest you shall be saved; in quietness and trust shall be your strength,'"(Is. 30:15).

Masculine: Patriarchy has received something of a bad press in recent times yet it forms the basis of the three Abrahamic religions: Judaism, Christianity, and Islam. In the Old Testament God is never referred to as female and in the New Testament when Jesus is asked to teach His disciples to pray, He instructs them in the "Our Father." That cultural and sociological imprint on spiritual development has largely shaped the way in which such development is formulated. Much of the literature on prayer and spiritual development was written for monks and by monks. Even the beautiful works written by women have the hallmark of masculine rather than feminine values: Masculine qualities include (at risk of sounding stereotypical) virility and strength (from the Latin *vir* meaning man), active, assertive, aggressive, courageous, bold decisive, dominant and forceful. By contrast, feminine qualities (again at risk of sounding stereotypical) include passive, receptive, cooperative, relational, collaborative intuitive and communicative.

The Godhead in Christianity is exclusively masculine: the Father, the Son and presumably, the Holy Ghost. The scriptures, both Jewish and Christian, are written by men. The twelve apostles are all male and in order to be a disciple one must be male for we read in the gospel of Matthew: "Then Jesus told his disciples, "If any man would come after me, let him deny himself and take up his cross and follow me." (Mt. 16:24). The leaders of the Catholic Church and the Church of England are both male and until fairly recently the clergy in the Church of England were all male. However, what is significant is that the Word became flesh through the body of a woman. God chose to take human form through Mary of Nazareth, without whom the Word would not have become flesh. We remember that much of the sublime writing on spirituality comes to us from women such as Dame Julian of Norwich and Teresa of Avila. We remember too that the development of Christianity was conditioned by historical rather than spiritual factors. We can take heart too by the knowledge that although we haven't, as yet, achieved full equality between women and men, we are on the road towards sexual equality always under the gentle, all-inclusive gaze of God.

Writings on the spiritual life have been largely dominated by qualities and values which favour an aggressive approach as witnessed by Paul's athletic analogy in 1 Corinthians. An alternative approach views life as something to be nurtured, not forced. It demands passive rather than active qualities, those traditionally understood as feminine. "The kingdom of God is as if a man should scatter seed upon the ground and should sleep and rise night and day, and the seed should sprout and grow, he knows not how" (Mk. 4:26-27).

Marked by self-denial: Traditional wisdom maintains that the higher reaches of prayer are attained through asceticism, abstinence and austerity. Fed on a diet of self-abnegation and self-denial, it is understandable that there can be little pleasure in exploring the highways and byways of the spiritual journey. In *The Ladder of Perfection*, Walter Hilton's 14th -century introduction to contemplative prayer, he writes

> By meditation shalt thou come to see thy wretchedness, thy sins and thy wickedness; as pride, covetousness, gluttony, sloth and lechery, wicked stirrings of envy, anger, hatred, melancholy, wrath, bitterness and imprudent heaviness, thy heart to be full of vain flames and fears of the flesh and of the world. All these stirrings will always boil out of thy heart, as water runneth out of the spring of a stinking well, and do hinder the sight of thy soul, that thou mayest never see nor feel clearly the love of Jesus Christ, for know thou well that until the heart be much cleansed from such sins, through firm

verity and diligent meditating on Christ's humanity, thou
canst not have any perfect knowledge of God.[24]

Reading that, I feel an itch to be flippant and wonder why, in such a catalogue of woes, there is no mention of simony, cruelty to animals or tax evasion. However, such a view of spiritual development has a long and revered history, and its Christian origins may be traced to Scripture. In the literature on spiritual development, much is made of the injunction to "enter by the narrow gate; for the way is easy that leads to destruction and those who enter by it are many. For the gate is narrow and the way is hard that leads to life." (Mt. 7:13, 14). In the third century, Origen went a little too far in his insistence that the only way to union with God was through purification from all passions and, as a consequence, made himself a eunuch for the kingdom of God by gelding himself. In a similar vein but without such disastrous self-mutilation, Cassian in the fifth century writes, "The end of all our perfection is thus so to act that the soul, stripping itself daily of all earthly and carnal inclinations, lifts itself up without

---

[24] W. Hilton, *The Scale of Perfection* (Scanned and edited by Harry Plantinga). This e-text is in the public domain, Chapter XIV, First Book, Part 1, 1995} 37.

ceasing more and more towards spiritual things."[25] Henry Suso, mentioned earlier, was merciless in subjecting his body to all manner of physical insults, scourging, fasting, and sleep-deprivation. If the rigours of mortification and self-denial are prerequisites for a life of prayer, it is little wonder that so few are prepared to embark on the journey.

We shall look at the process of purification when we come to visit the first of the properties of the gaze of God. Suffice it to say here that the example which Paul gives in his first letter to the Corinthians forms a rationale for an approach to spiritual growth based on self-denial using the analogy of athletic training he writes, "I pommel my body and subdue it, lest after preaching to others I myself should be disqualified" (1Cor. 9:27). In Romans, he complains "For I delight in the law of God in my inmost self; but I see in my members another law at war with the law of my mind and making me captive to the law of sin which dwells in my members" (Rm. 7:23); in Galatians he writes, "Walk by the Spirit and do not gratify the desires of the flesh" (Gal. 5:17).

---

[25] John Cassian, in M.Cox, *Mysticism: The Direct Experience of God.* (Aquarian Press, 1983).

These verses demonstrate a way of understanding spiritual development based on a view which holds that there is a dichotomy between body and soul, that the body as matter is prone to evil, and the spirit is unphysical and yearns to be united with God. We read in Paul's letter to the Romans that the two are in constant conflict. Through a process of asceticism, the body with its ruling passions is to be made subservient to the spirit.

Ascetical practices continued through the early Church with Pachomius, Anthony, and the Desert Fathers and Mothers and found its most grotesque expression in the Middle Ages, particularly among women: Catherine of Siena was a prime example of distorted practices. Reinforced by the personal pact with God, Catherine entered into battle with her family. She lost half of her proper weight and opposed the demands of her mother by fasting which confirmed her true dedication to God, and renouncing her "corporeality"[26] at the expense, it should be added, of filial piety. There was a struggle of wills between Catherine and her mother who wished her to marry the widower of her recently deceased sister. Catherine fasted

---

[26] R.M. Bell, *Holy Anorexics* (Chicago University Press, 1985) 50.

perhaps more as a way of retaliation against her mother than for any spiritual motive. To lose half one's body weight is the result not of fasting but what has come to be called *anorexia mirabilis,* which was frequently coupled with other ascetic practices, such as lifelong virginity, flagellant behaviour, the donning of hair shirts, sleeping on beds of thorns and other assorted self-mutilations. Distortions in self-perception and a streak of stubbornness lie at the root of the excesses of Catherine and many other young women in the Middle Ages. However, it must be stated that Catherine achieved wisdom and sanctity despite these practices and would be better served were her love for God acknowledged above her egregious penitential practices.

Catherine's self-perception and understanding of God was fallible possibly because she failed to recognise how she came to be as a person. The process by which the self develops is one of gradual separation out of an original mother-infant matrix, a process by which the child begins to differentiate between what Winnicott labels the "me" from the "not-me." The process begins with attachment and moves towards individuation. The infant, made up of a complex psyche-soma relationship embarks on a growth towards integration of the psyche-soma which forms a regulatory mechanism of the self. When the process of differentiation is disturbed in any way through deficiencies in mothering, integration fails to take place, and as a consequence of these deficiencies, self-mutilation and disordered eating habits may sometimes become instruments by which the individual attempts to regulate the self. When one adds into the mix a cultural and philosophical acceptance of the wickedness of the flesh and the assumption that the only way to achieve sanctity is to mortify the flesh in order to purify the spirit, then one is faced with not one but two distortions in perception of the self on its way to God.

Under the gaze of God, there are three considerations which militate against an approach to spiritual growth based on extreme asceticism: The first is that the orientation is towards the self rather than towards the face of God; there is a preoccupation with personal faults, failings, and sins, and self takes centre stage. The second consideration is the assumption that by the practice of Christian asceticism, one can pull oneself up by the proverbial bootlaces and achieve union with God. Of course, the spiritual writers of antiquity were aware of this danger. John of the Cross writes, "One must greatly lament the ignorance of some men, who burden themselves with extraordinary penances and with many other voluntary practices, and think that this practice or that will suffice to bring them to the union of Divine Wisdom; but such will not be the case if they endeavour not diligently to mortify their desires."[27] This caution, however, did not seem to act as a brake for those who continued and continue to advocate a path of self-denial, mortification, and abstention from physical pleasure. Thirdly, such an approach is profoundly negative. Mortification, by definition, is focused on death and, as such, is a profound denial of life. Further, if we are motivated by fear, constantly looking over our shoulder, afraid of being called to account for real or imagined failings, then it is inevitable that the way is lost because we are moving in one direction and looking over our shoulder in the opposite direction. If we lose sight of the face of God, we are bound to go astray.

---

[27] John of the Cross, *Ascent of Mount Carmel,* Translated and Edited by E Allison Peers, revised edition, (The Newman Press, 1953, Bk 1, Ch. VIII) 40-41.

I believe that the whole point of the Adam and Eve story is not that it tells, in Milton's words, "Of Man's first disobedience, and the fruit of that forbidden tree whose mortal taste Brought death into the World, and all our woe," but a story of reconciliation and comforting. Adam and Eve were cowering in the undergrowth before the approach of God, but they are drawn out of hiding by his compassionate gaze. Much of the beauty of the story lies in the fact that this God is one who sits down and knits them aprons to cover their nakedness. How like a mother!

Perhaps the way of looking at spiritual progress as one based on mortification and self-denial is the reason why there are no portraits of smiling mystics; still less are mystics portrayed as doubled over with laughter. One would think that union with God is so blissful, so delightful, literally so ecstatic that it would be impossible to suppress a grin, but apparently not. Of course, if one had been kidnapped, imprisoned, and beaten, locked in a tiny cell without light, as was John of the Cross, then there would be little to laugh about.

Again, why are mystics so intense? In his foreword to Iain Matthew's splendid book on John of the Cross, Jean Vanier refers to John as "John of Pain,"[28] which he views approvingly because, for him, it provides a corrective to a view of Jesus which Vanier maintains is far too familiar and cosy, a view which robs Jesus of his divinity and sacredness. Yet if God went to such inordinate trouble to become one with us, warts and all; if God cast aside His dignity to get down on hands and knees and play with His children, why should we not take Him at His word?

I am often asked, "Why does prayer have to be so hard? Why so difficult?" This book is an attempt to reassure and comfort those who pose such questions with the reply, "It doesn't need to be so hard." This is not being glib. Obviously, there are difficulties; pain and grief, which is often inconsolable, difficulties which form part of human experience. Built into the human condition is an unavoidable capacity for suffering; it comes with the territory, yet I submit that the normal suffering we are heir to is more than sufficient in itself as a means of refining the spirit without adding unnecessary pain. Heartache, disappointment, grief, failure, despair are inevitable, and when interpreted under the gaze of

---

[28] I. Matthew, *The Impact of God* (Hodder and Stoughton, 1995) xi.

1

God become a crucible in which the Spirit is purified. (But more of that later.)

A dynamic perspective on spiritual development, as mentioned earlier, involves two movements, the first being a movement of return. The movement of return is one of *metanoia*, a process of conversion, which involves a succession of movements leading towards integration and wholeness. These movements are movements of growth and have little, if anything to do with repentance for sin. Gustavo Gutierrez in his book *A Theology of Liberation* notes, "Conversion is a permanent process in which very often the obstacles we meet make us lose all we had gained thus far and start anew. The fruitfulness of our conversion depends on our openness to doing this, our spiritual childhood."[29]

The subtitle of this book, *Perspectives on Spiritual Development*, provides the literary structure in which we shall examine a variety of different ways of looking at spiritual development, mainly from the viewpoint of psychology. Chapter 1 reflects on the nature and structure of trust, drawing on some of the insights of developmental

---

[29] G. Gutierrez, *A Theology of Liberation* (SCM Press, 1981) 205.

psychology, with particular reference to the first of Erik Erikson's stages of psychosocial development. At this initial stage, infant negotiates the developmental task of resolving the tension between trust and mistrust. Trust lies at the very foundation of any human relationship and even more so our relationship with God. Trust will be considered as having three orientations: towards process; presence; efficacy; and then consideration will be given to the opposite side of the coin, namely, mistrust, where a healthy suspicion of feelings is advocated. Within the first object of trust, attention will be paid to four movements of conversion: from active to passive; from impersonal to personal; from insensitivity to sensitivity; from a desire for control towards surrender. Trust is essentially the gateway to hope. Chapter 2 will reflect on the nature and dynamics of hope, drawing on some of the insights of the philosophy of history and citing examples from the prophetic experience of the Old Testament. Chapter 2 examines the dynamics of hope, where hope is understood to be rooted in the ground of human becoming. Chapter 3 will address the dynamics of return, of that perpetual movement of conversion into which we are drawn by the gaze of God. This movement will also reflect spiritual development as mirroring human growth and will focus on a series of movements towards spiritual maturity, relying on some dimensions of maturation proposed by Knowles.[30] It involves a series of conversions: away from self-rejection towards self-acceptance; away from a need for certainty towards a tolerance of ambiguity; away from primitive need towards desire; from dependence to autonomy. Once the foundations of trust, hope, and conversion are laid, it is time, in Chapter 4 to explore the dynamics of the desert experience in prayer, for the wilderness is the locus of liberation as was the experience of Israel as a child. It is into the wilderness that we are seduced by the voice of God Who chooses the barren wastes as the place where He speaks tenderly to the human heart.

All the while development is taking place under the warm gaze of God who, like the sun, brings light and growth to the human spirit. Chapter 5 will therefore focus first of all upon light which is the origin of life for all living creatures before addressing the effects which the gaze of the living God brings

---

[30] M. S. Knowles, *The Modern Practice of Adult Education*, (New York, Association Press, 1970) 25.

about in the human spirit. Returning to John of the Cross and the *Canticle,* I shall draw on the properties which John assigns to the gaze of God: "For the better understanding of what has been said, and of what follows, it must be known that the look of God works four blessings in the soul, namely, that it cleanses, beautifies, enriches and enlightens it, even as the sun, when it sends forth its rays, dries and warms and beautifies and makes resplendent." In line with the dynamic and elliptical nature of the book, the four blessings which the gaze of God confers upon the soul are set in the context of the rhythm of the seasons. The blessing of cleansing is presented as a winter blessing; the blessing of making beautiful is shown to be the blessing of springtime; the third blessing, that of enrichment, is seen as the blessing of summer; and, finally, the blessing of enlightenment is the rich blessing of autumn.

Chapter 1

First Perspective

Trust – The Wellspring of Connectedness

It is a fearful thing to fall into the hands of the living God.
But it is a much more fearful thing to fall out of them.
D.H.Lawrence

Trust is the primary and foundational achievement of human and spiritual development; it differs from faith in that trust is both experiential and relational. Faith may also be seen as relational but it has the component of intellectual assent which is missing in trust. In *Identity, Youth and Crisis* Erik Erikson presents a schema of eight developmental challenges which span human life from infancy to late adulthood.[1] The first of these challenges occurs in the first eighteen months of life and has to do with how the infant negotiates and resolves the tension between trust and mistrust. When the mother provides food, warmth, shelter and comfort and communicates

---

[1]   A more complete treatment of this schema is to be found in his book *Childhood and Society*

1

with her baby, then the baby begins to view the environment as friendly, supportive and worthy of trust. When, by contrast, the basic needs of infants are not met, they grow uncertain, doubtful and suspicious, viewing the environment as hostile. Consequently, they will withdraw into themselves and fail to form interactive, empathetic responses which are imperative for the development of a healthy emotional life and, more crucially, the development of a healthy spiritual life. Infants not only depend on their mother for the basic provisions of life: food, warmth, shelter, communication, contact, they also depend on the mother for something equally important. A sense of trust is built primarily upon the foundation of one of the most important and natural expressions of care which the mother provides for her baby. Quite simply, she holds her infant. Physical touch is essential for the communication of life: bees pollinate flowers through touch; eggs are fertilised by touch; we were conceived through touch; we blossom into humanness through the warm touch of others; the healing miracles of Jesus are largely performed through his touch. Silverman notes, "With birth the initial and continued physical closeness of infants and mothers is essential for healthy growth

2

and adaptation of infants."[2] She cites the work of Barnes on the significant biological impact touch has on infant growth and development. "Depriving infants of maternal contact", Silverman writes, "will lead to weight deficiency and damage normal development. Premature babies can overcome maturational lags and flourish through physical handling and solicitous care."[3] Touch is primary and foundational because by holding her baby, the mother introduces the infant to the experience of what it is like to be loved, that experience from which all subsequent experiences of love both human and divine are derived. We are loved because we have first been held and we grow to trust our environment to the degree to which we are loved, and to that same degree, we come to rely on the environment as basically friendly.

In 1945, René Spitz, an Austrian psychoanalyst, did research on children in their first year of life in an orphanage. He found that the babies were well cared for: they were fed, changed and kept warm and comfortable but he noticed that

---

[2] D K Silverman, "Attachment Research. An Approach to a Developmental Relational Perspective." In *Relational Perspectives in Psychoanalysis*, Neill J. Skolnick and Susan C. Warshaw (The Analytic Press, 1992) 200–201.

[3] Silverman, "Attachment Research 201.

they failed to thrive. Not only did they fail to thrive, but they became withdrawn, some curling up in the foetal position and some, even more tragically, not surviving the first year of life. Spitz discovered that the reason the infants failed to thrive was simply because they weren't held or cuddled.[4]

Physical touch and holding is vital for emotional development not only because it provides the basic experience of being loved but also because it meets an equally important need: that of protection from anxiety. Holding protects the baby from being exposed to unthinkable anxiety. Winnicott writes:

> It is necessary to postulate a stage, which belongs to inter-uterine life, in which gravity has not yet appeared; love or care can only be expressed and appreciated in physical terms, in environmental adaptation which is applied from all directions. One of the changes brought about by the birth of the child is that the newborn infant has to adapt to something quite new, which is the experience of being pushed up from below instead of held all round. The infant changes from being loved from all directions to being loved from below only.... Clumsiness in regard to the management of this change from the pre-gravitational to the gravitational era gives a basis to the dream of falling forever.[5]

---

[4] R A Spitz, *The First Year of Life: A Psychoanalytic Study of Normal and Deviant Development of Object Relations* (New York: International Universities Press, 1965).

[5] D W Winnicott, *Human Nature* (New York: Scholoken Books, 1988) 130.

Babies in their early months of life cannot hold their head erect, cannot walk, cannot even crawl; they are dependent on secure holding and this acts as a bulwark, a defence against unimaginable primitive anxiety. If they are not held securely, confusion and anxiety set in. Quite literally, babies exposed to this kind of environ-mental failure have been let down and will spend most of their lives subsequently building defences against the primitive agonies by which they have been traumatised. As a consequence, they grow into adulthood suspicious and critical of the environment and find it difficult, if not impossible, to build sustaining and rewarding relationships, least of all with God.

As we go back to the beginning of life outside the womb, so too we may go back to the beginning of life in the book of Genesis. It is no accident that the sin of Adam and Eve is described as "the Fall", because here we have something which is primitive, grounded in the earliest days of human life. From birth, as noted above, we need to be held and supported because one of our most primitive fears is that of falling, and our falling leads to the disintegration of the self. This fear finds expression in the popular phrases such as "falling down on the job", "falling apart at the seams," and "falling to pieces." We use this image across a variety of different contexts because it is such a powerful symbol of our insecurity. Why do so many people surround themselves with more than they need if not to build defences against their own insecurity and to bolster their self-worth? Insurance companies are built on the premise of the universality of human insecurity and frailty and some of their policies are designed to act as a hedge against falling into debt.

We use the metaphor of the fall to describe overwhelming physical attraction; we call it "falling in love". This speaks to the situation where control is lost. I am not in control; I have lost a sense of who I am. I can't eat, can't sleep; all thoughts are on the beloved. Fortunately, it doesn't last very long. Yet again, the metaphorical fall describes a diminishment of the self. "Falling down on the job" means that we do not measure up to the expectations of others. I have let myself and others down and my own sense of self-worth is diminished in my eyes. In days gone by, we used to use the phrase "fallen into sin" to mean a loss of integrity, a loss of one's own spiritual worth. Nursery rhymes which formed part of childhood brought face to face with the fear of falling: "Rock-a-bye Baby" and "Humpty Dumpty" are but two. There is something atavistic in these rhymes, echoing as they do the primal fear to which we are all heirs.

To some degree, we bear within us vestiges of that primal fear for the simple reason that mothers, or fathers for that matte are human and, as such, fallible. We all bear preconscious memories of not having our most basic needs met, of not being fed precisely when we needed to be fed; of unpleasant and cold wetness when we needed to be changed; of being startled by a car's backfire in the street but most frightening of all, preconscious memories of being held insecurely which results in a situation in which we are hesitant to trust. These hesitancies have become ingrained deep within our psyches, embedded in our sense of self, and express themselves most acutely when we are confronted with situations of insecurity.

Prayer is an experience which confronts us with insecurity in face of the unknown. When we place ourselves in the presence of a God we cannot see, hear, or touch and many of those insecurities rise to the surface and trouble us with the notion that perhaps, after all, we do not trust God as much as we'd like to. This is part of the fragmented human condition that we place, in all its frailty and nakedness, to be exposed to the gaze of God when we come to prayer. No wonder that Adam and Eve sought shelter in the undergrowth when they heard the voice of God.

Resurrection faith offers the possibility of countering these hesitancies. "For he will give his angels charge over you, to guard you in all your ways. On their hands they will bear you up, lest you dash your foot against a stone" (Ps. 91: 11, 12). We are held by the angels of God when our deepest fears, anxieties, and worries form a dark cloud which only the light of Christ can penetrate. If we are truly children of the Resurrection, people of faith, grounded in the conviction that no matter what happens, no matter what sorrow or tragedy arrives at the doorstep of our souls, we are always held in the hands of God, and no one will ever snatch us out of the hands of the living God, the hand of love. "It is a fearful thing to fall into the hands of the living God. But it is a much more fearful thing to fall out of them."[6]

---

[6]   D.H. Lawrence, *The Hands of the Living God,* Edited by Vivian de Sola Pinto and Warren Roberts (Harmondsworth, Middlesex: Penguin Books, 1991) 699.

There is another facet of human nature which faces us with the challenge to trust. This is a property which lies at the very heart of what it means to be human; it differentiates us from other mammals. We differ from cows and sheep not only because we have larger brains, not only because we are self-aware, not only because we have a sense of time and history, but because essentially we are unfinished. We are and always will be a work in progress. Whereas lesser mammals have a biologically determined relationship to their environment, humans by their nature are open-ended; their relationship to their environment is one of what Berger and Luckmann term "world-openness." They write, "Not only has man succeeded in establishing himself over the greater part of the earth's surface, his relationship to the surrounding environment is everywhere very imperfectly structured by his own biological constitution."[7] Cats don't have to go to school to learn how to chase mice; dogs don't need a university degree to know how to chase cats. By contrast, we have to learn how to become human. Obviously, we are endowed with certain instinctual

---

[7] P. I. Berger and T. Luckmann, *The Social Construction of Reality* (Harmondsworth: Penguin Books, 1971) 65.

forces, such as sex, aggression and self-preservation but our relationship to the environment is a loose one and one which includes the element of choice. When choice enters in, so do uncertainty and perplexity. Shall I have prawn cocktail or soup to start? And when I have made my choice, I wonder what it would have been like to have chosen the other option and a note of dissatisfaction potentially enters in. The non-specificity of our instinctual constitution brings with it an awareness that not only are we in danger of falling, we are also in danger of being swamped by a deluge of potential choices. Choice brings with it the possibility of uncertainty, and for those of us who have a propensity for self-doubt, choice opens the door to uncertainty and disquiet.

We now turn from the abstract to a more concrete approach to the subject of trust and adopt an experiential approach to the ways in which trust forms the foundation of spiritual development. Ways in which trust discloses itself will be treated under the following headings: 1. Trust in the process of spiritual development; 2. Trust in the presence of the living

God; 3. Trust in the efficacy of prayer. And, by contrast, 4. Healthy mistrust: trust is always held in tension with mistrust and even for reasons of self-preservation, a response of mistrust is sometimes to be preferred to trust because some people always try to take advantage of the gullible.

1. Trust in the process

Sometimes, people will say, ruefully or with a sense of self-criticism, "I haven't progressed very far in my prayer life." If they embarked on a journey, they want to know where they are going and how long it will take. Understandable really but it does tend to put the brake on spiritual growth. Spiritual development like biological growth is a process of maturation, constantly evolving, constantly moving. Confronted with the reality of growth as process, we have to be patient; we have to let it happen. "The kingdom of God is as if a man should scatter seed upon the ground, and should sleep and rise night and day, and the seed should sprout and grow, he knows not how, the earth produces of itself, first the blade, then the ear, then the full grain in the ear" (Mk. 4:26-28). In a similar vein, George Vaillant, in his book *Adaptation to Life,* reflects on the manner in which healing takes place and notes the importance of standing back and allowing the process to unfold without interfering. "One of the great advances of modern [nineteenth-century] surgery was to recognize that nothing could be done to hasten wound healing except to understand it well enough to learn how not to stand in the way."[8] Spiritual growth happens if we allow it to happen and refrain from impeding its development by trying to determine how far along the path we have progressed. Perhaps we should take to heart the sentiment Paul expresses in his letter to the Philippians: "Indeed I count everything as loss because of the surpassing worth of knowing Christ Jesus my Lord. For his sake I have suffered the loss of all things, and count them as refuse, in order that I may gain Christ" (Phil. 3:8). Spiritual development, growth and healing are not something that we do; they unfold gradually under the creative gaze of the living God. All we have to do is turn up, spend twenty or thirty minutes each day in the presence of God and let Him do the rest. Woody Allen is reputed to have said that 80per cent of success is just turning

---

8 G.E. Vaillant, *Adaptation to Life,* (Boston, Toronto: Little, Brown and Co. 1977) 369.

up. There may well be some truth in that. This is not meant to imply that we do not need some help along the way or that there are no signposts and markers which merit our attention. Of course there are. There are two observations which alert us to the nature of our progress along the path to union with God and they concern the second and third ways trust becomes operative on our path: trust in the presence of the living God and trust in the efficacy of prayer; in other words, becoming more sensitive to the way the effects of prayer influence, colour and shape our reactions and responses to other people and how those effects help to determine how we deal with the petty annoy-ances of daily life. But before proceeding to a consideration of the second and third ways trust is actualised, there is more work to be done on the dynamics of the process of spiritual development.

In my work as a spiritual director, I treasure those God-touched moments when I have been privileged to witness the flowering of the human spirit as people respond to God revealing Himself. I notice how they become more still, yet more alive; quieter yet more present; more assured yet more vulnerable; sharing on a deeper, more authentic level, and at these times, I experience the touch of God, the thrill of knowing, deep within, that this indeed is a precious moment. I stand, indeed, on holy ground. It is as if someone has placed a finger on my heart and my heart jumps at the touch. It is a moment of such incredible intimacy that I find myself holding my breath in case any movement or word of mine might break the spell.

I ask myself where does it come from or what is happening or what is God doing here and I find that I come, little by little, to an awareness of what is happening, how one individual is moving away from intense activity towards a less frenetic lifestyle or how another person's relationship with God is changing from a distant, rather impersonal relationship, into something far more real, far more personal, far more intimate. Another person will describe how her social life has taken an upswing and how she finds she has far more time for people nowadays; another will describe how he is more aware of what God is doing in his daily life outside his time of prayer.

Reflecting on and praying over these experiences in the process of spiritual growth towards maturity which I have been privileged to witness over the years, I have traced certain predictable lines of growth. For simplicity's sake, I have narrowed these lines down to four: the movement from activity to passivity; from the impersonal to the personal (a movement which includes growth away from the abstract towards the concrete); from insensitivity towards an increased awareness of the effects of prayer on daily life; movement from a desire to control towards a freedom of surrender. These movements demonstrate a change of position, a movement of return to the place where we started; the movement from activity to passivity is a movement back to our original state, to a time when we were totally receptive and any action on our part was designed to elicit, in whatever primitive fashion we were able, a response to which we could become receptive.

The second developmental movement, from the impersonal to the personal, draws us, as Martin Buber points out, away from an "I-It" to an "I-Thou" relation-ship, one which we enjoyed at our mother's breast. There is a subset to this particular movement, one of moving from abstract to concrete which draws us back to a world without abstraction for the simple reason that we were incapable of abstract thought when we were infants. Everything was concrete, much as it is for monkeys and wolves.

The third movement is towards an increasing sensitivity to and awareness of the way the Spirit moves and acts in the everyday and the humdrum. The fourth, but by no means final, movement is perhaps the most difficult because it demands a letting go of a need for control, of a compulsion to be in charge and necessitates a movement towards that surrender of self which brings us closer to union with God.

At this juncture, I need to mention that these four ways in which the life-force of conversion unfolds lie nested and embedded in larger lines of development which will be discussed in a subsequent chapter. To return to the four lines of development, we begin with consideration of the first movement, that of moving from an active way of being towards a more receptive stance.

(a) From activity to passivity

This major line of spiritual development follows a process I describe as one of "gentling." In two people I have walked with - one a diocesan priest, the other a religious sister – I noticed a distinct change. In both priest and sister there emerged a more reflective quality to their sharing; they were somewhat surprised at their slowing down and less caught up in the hustle and bustle of their daily lives:

> I don't know what it is, but these days I seem to be doing less work, but I seem to be getting more done. Isn't it strange? Not so long ago, I can remember rushing around and fretting if I didn't get everything finished. Now it doesn't seem to matter so much ... it is as if the Lord is saying to me that it is His work, not mine, and He'll take care of everything.
> Religious Sister[9]

> When I used to get a call to the hospital, I would jump in my car like a madman and get there as soon as I could, but what I tend to do now is just put the person in the hands of God, and I stop and think of what I am about to do, and I sorta ask the Lord to be with me, and it seems that we both go to the hospital together ... and I find that at other times too ... I don't rush around quite so much ... I realise better that everything does not depend on me, and that kinda removes the pressure ... and I notice if I don't give time to prayer, then I seem to fall back into the old ways of doing things ... I don't take exercise, and my blood pressure goes way up because I'm trying to do too much.
> Diocesan Priest

As a result of their willingness to spend time in prayer, they slow the pace of life down. They both become aware that the

---

[9] All the citations in this section are taken from transcripts of sessions of spiritual direction at the Center for Religious Development, Cambridge, MA, from 1985 to 1986.

quality of life improves and "that removes the pressure"; they find that they can enjoy their work more. Old habits, however, die hard, and they need, as do we all, to be reminded from time to time of their insight into the working of the Spirit in their lives.

(b) From the impersonal to the personal

Again, this is a movement of return to that state we enjoyed as infants, to the time when, for us, the impersonal didn't exist. Central to my own faith understanding lies the strong belief that God constantly communicates Himself to us and calls us into intimate union with Him, so it is that I am saddened when someone shares with me an understanding of a God Who is aloof, distant and impersonal, and although I do nothing to impose my own understanding of God (for all our understandings of Him are, in the last analysis, projections), I am heartened if there is a sign of movement towards a more personal relationship with the Lord.

An example of this kind of conversion may be seen from one woman's experience. When she first came for direction, she said that she wanted some sort of symbol she could use as a focus for her prayer. She described how she went to buy a cross; she didn't want a crucifix because she didn't want to face an image of Jesus. It surfaced in subsequent conversations that she had had a difficult relationship with her husband, who divorced her after only eighteen months of marriage and who subsequently committed suicide. These experiences left her scarred and she explained that for her, it was impossible to enter into any sort of relationship with any degree of intimacy. She then described how she changed as a result of something which happened while on a retreat in New York. I quote her experience at some length in order to provide a more complete picture of what she went through.

> I was really tired when I arrived at the place. I flew down to New York after work on Friday, then I had to get the limousine, and they said that they would pick me up at the mall. There must have been a mix-up because there was no car there when I arrived. It was pouring with rain, and I felt cold and miserable. Eventually, someone came and took me to the retreat house. By this time, it was about ten o'clock, and they, that is, the other people on retreat were all in the chapel, so I thought I would go and join them.... I wasn't really hungry and I didn't want to miss any of the retreat sessions.... When I got to the chapel, the place was in darkness except for two candles which were standing on the floor. There was a huge crucifix lying on the floor in front of the altar, and the service, or whatever it was, was just coming to an end. I just sat there at the back of the chapel while all the others left. Although I was tired, I felt a sense of peace. I was sort of cosy and comfortable, and I sat there for a time. Then I felt drawn to go up to the crucifix. I kept my

eyes on the feet because I didn't want to look at the face, and I felt a struggle going on within me. I wanted to, and I didn't want to at the same time. It was quite a wrench, but I forced myself to look up. I sort of made myself look up slowly from the feet all the way up this body until I sat looking at the face ... the eyes looked straight at me, and I just burst into tears.... I sat there and sobbed and sobbed. It was all right, I felt that here was someone who loved me so much, and it seemed that a cold place inside me had been warmed.

Out of this experience, there unfolded within her a familiarity, previously unknown, with Jesus; she found it increasingly easy to talk to Him at odd moments during the day. Further, she says that she has derived a great richness from her growing relationship with Jesus.

Movement from the impersonal to the personal is one of the more important forms of conversion because it is, by definition, a movement which turns from experience-distant to experience-near; from impersonal to intimate; from public to private; from lifeless to vibrant. Rudolph Bultmann, in his book *Jesus and the Word,* writes

If a man must say that he cannot find God in the reality of his own present life, and if he would compensate for this by the thought that God is nevertheless the final cause of all that happens, then his belief in God will be a theoretical speculation or a dogma; and however great the force with which he clings to this belief, it will not be true faith, for faith can be only the recognition of the activity of God in his own life.[10]

Change of heart implies a movement away from thinking about God as "the final cause of all that happens" to "the recognition of the activity of God in his own life." Aldous Huxley writes

> If we approach God with the preconceived idea that He is exclusively the personal, transcendental, all-powerful ruler of the world, we run the risk of becoming entangled in a religion of rites, propitiatory sacrifices (sometimes of the most horrible nature) and legalistic observances.... The best that can be said for ritualistic legalism is that it improves conduct.... Things are a great deal better when the transcendent, omnipotent personal God is regarded as also a loving Father.[11]

The movement from ritual to relationship involves a movement from head to heart, for God is not attained through thinking but through a powerfully affective response to a call. In other words, we need a radical shift of emphasis in how we relate to God. Such movement is a challenge to let go of an understanding of God based on structures or ecclesiastic authority; these external influences do not penetrate the

---

[10] R. Bultmann, *Jesus and the Word.* Translated by L P Smith and E H Lantero (Fontana, 1958) 113.

[11] A. Huxley, *The Perennial Philosophy*, (New York, London: Harper Perennial Modern Classics, 2009) 23.

innermost recesses of the human spirit. By contrast, the call is to take up a contemplative stance before the God Who calls us into a deep and intimate relationship. It is a call to a movement towards authenticity where we may claim our own authority before God and assume responsibility for life. Because we are human, however, affected by life experiences which have wounded us, movement of this sort usually carries with it anxieties stemming from a basic insecurity.

(c) Towards a sensitivity to the Spirit's prompting in daily life

Sometimes, (or frequently in Mother Teresa's case), one finds prayer time to be restless, apparently sterile, even desolate. At those times, we look at our watch to gauge the passage of time, only to wonder if the watch has stopped. What is the point of it all? Little consolation is to be found in these words of St Teresa: "Prayer is the ability to waste time gracefully with God." Those seeds, planted in the dark and restless heart, bear fruit in ways perhaps we least expect. We may notice something different in the way we react to other people. Waiting in line at the checkout counter, there's an elderly woman in front who is fumbling in her bag for her purse, then she fumbles in her purse for her money, and with painful slowness, she puts some coins in the check-out girl's hand. She then peers into the girl's hand and takes back some of the coins and replaces them with other coins.

The woman takes what seems an eternity to pay for her groceries, and this would ordinarily induce spasms of profound irritation, yet with a gentle sigh, we commend the lady to heaven, where previously we may well have consigned her to hell. Empathy for an elderly woman, perhaps lonely, perhaps confused, rises to the surface and we experience the peace which surpasses all understanding. That is the fruit of prayer. Fruit is borne in places we least expect; sometimes it is only God having some fun at our expense.

Because we are social animals, prayer, if we allow it and if we are sensitive to its movements, will always have an influence on the way we interact with others.

As one woman in direction put it:

> I live in a small town, well, it's little more than a village really, and I always kept myself pretty much to myself … it's not that I am unsociable or anything, it's just that I have never done much entertaining … well, one thing which I noticed and that is I am far more open to people than I used to be. Take the other day, for instance. The sheriff came round, apparently there had been a series of

burglaries in the neighbourhood, and he just wanted to warn me about them. Normally, I would thank him for his trouble and that would be that. This time, I invited him in, and he sat on the edge of the kitchen table, and we had quite a long chat.... He told me about his family, and we got into some pretty heavy stuff about the meaning of life ... can you imagine that! Then when he left, a neighbour of mine called round, and we had a long talk ... it was only that night when I thought about what had happened, and I came to realise that it is all due to the time I am spending in prayer ... it has made such a difference ... *people are beginning to matter to me in a way that they didn't before.* (italics added)

Because we are human and capable of self-deception, a note of caution must be added. Sometimes, the connection between what appears to happen in prayer and the events of daily life outside prayer time is not always clear. One woman confided how she was standing at the bus stop and saw a homeless woman rooting around in the bin; she said she felt a strong urge to approach her and tell her all about Jesus. It seemed terribly important that she should convey this message that Jesus loves her. When asked what she did, she replied.

I didn't go over to her, and I could hear this voice ordering me to go over to her ... it was insistent and imperious and demanding, and it made me feel quite upset.

When I asked her if this was the way she normally experienced God communicating to her, she replied that

24

normally she experienced a certain calm, which was at odds with the stridency of the inner voice she heard. On further questioning, she was able to appreciate the difference between impulses which were of divine origin and those which emanated from the shadow side of her own personality. There is a world of difference between the gentling process by which the God-Mother soothes the spirit and the harsh, imperious tones of the shadow side which former generations projected onto the devil and his angels.

(d) From a need to control to surrender of self

This movement occurs as a result of confrontation. This particular confrontation faces us with the necessity of abandoning our need for certainty and allowing ourselves to be nakedly addressed by The Other Who cannot be confined or imprisoned or reduced to the narrow limits of our vision. In short, the movement is a call to abandon any temptation to domesticate God. It involves a radical shift of emphasis, one which leads to greater authenticity in our relationship with God and with one another, but one which, like all such experiences, is often distressing.

This movement demands trust because it requires the abandonment of a need to possess. Trust, in this instance, is the process of letting go and allowing God the freedom to act within our spirits. Etty Hillesum, born 13 January 1914, was a young Jewish woman who, like Ann Frank, kept diaries of life in the Netherlands during the German occupation. She was to lose her life in the gas chambers of Auschwitz on 30 November, 1943. The following extract illustrates her conversion away from possessiveness towards abandonment of self:

> And here I have hit upon something essential. Whenever I saw a beautiful flower, what I longed to do with it was press it to my heart, or eat it all up.... I yearned physically for all I thought was beautiful, wanted to own it. Hence that painful longing that could never be satisfied, the pining for something I thought unobtainable, which I called the creative urge ... it all suddenly changed, *God alone knows by what inner process.* I realised it only this morning when I recalled a short walk round the Skating Club a few nights ago. It was dusk, soft hues in the sky, mysterious silhouettes of houses, trees alive with the light through the tracery of their branches, in short, enchanting. And then I knew precisely how I had felt in the past. Then all that beauty would have gone like a stab to my heart, and I would not have known what to do with the pain. Then I would have felt the need to write, to compose verses, but the words would still have refused to come. I would have felt utterly miserable, wallowed in the pain and exhausted myself as a result. The experience would have sapped

all my energy. Now I know it for what it was: mental masturbation.

But that night, only just gone, *I reacted quite differently.* I felt that God's world was beautiful despite everything, but its beauty now filled me with joy. I was just as deeply moved by that mysterious, still landscape in the dusk as I might have been before, *but somehow I no longer wanted to own it.* I went home invigorated and went back to work (italics added)[12]

After this brief survey of some of the dynamics of spiritual growth and development, it is time to turn our attention to the second dimension of trust which calls for faithful response, namely, openness to God's abiding presence, the God Who gazes upon us with such fondness.

2. Trust in the presence of God

We grow in trust that God is always with us, to the degree that we are sensitised to His presence. And that comes with practice. When I was a novice in Broadway, Worcestershire, the novice master would take us for a walk every Thursday and Sunday afternoon. On the walk, one of the novices who was responsible for ringing the bells for the various daily offices that week would periodically remind us of the presence of

---

[12] E. Hillesum, *An Interrupted Life: The Diaries of Etty Hillesum, 1941-43* (New York, London: Washington Square Press, 1985) 13.

God. In those days, we were not allowed to wear wristwatches so the novice would cart around one of those old-fashioned alarm clocks, the ones with the huge metal bell on the top and every twenty minutes on the walk, he would call a halt and proclaim the presence of God, to which the next novice would proclaim, "Jesus and Mary be praised," to which we would all respond, "Forever and ever." At times, as you can imagine, it was acutely embarrassing, such as when we were in the middle of a busy high street but perhaps the embarrassment served to reinforce an awareness that God was truly present in the discomfort and embarrassment. The idea, presumably, was to get us into the habit (pun intended) of becoming increasingly aware of the all-abiding gracious presence of God, not only in chapel or in the cloister, but, even more significantly, on a street filled with busy shoppers.

It is an exercise I would strongly advocate, not carrying around a cumbersome alarm clock but setting a daily schedule of noting a time at intervals of thirty minutes or one hour when you call to mind that you are in the presence of a God Who is constantly gazing fondly upon you. It may be more helpful to set upon a time which doesn't coincide with the hour or half-hour. Choosing a time such as seven minutes past the hour seems to make it more urgent, and it makes us aware of a vague disappointment when we miss our appointment with God, so to speak, and resolve not to miss it the next time.

What this exercise also serves to promote is a sense of the constant presence of God. No matter where we are, no matter whom we are with, we become sensitised to the all-pervasive presence of the Trinity within us and enfolding us in the warmth of everlasting love. A very precious person gave me a gift after we suspended spiritual direction. The gift was a plaque containing the Latin words Carl Jung had carved over the front door of his house in Zurich: *Vocatus atque non vocatus Deus aderit* (Bidden or not bidden, God is present). We are constantly surrounded with evidence of God's presence but often our cares, preoccupations, routines and hang-ups form a veil which obscures His Presence. We are quite able to acknowledge the presence of God when we are exposed to the awesome majesty of a mountain, the wonder of a spectacular sunset, or the smile of a loved one; it is relatively easy to be beguiled by the beauty of poetry and music, to "see his blood upon the rose/ And in the stars the glory of his eyes" (Joseph

29

Mary Plunkett), but it is more difficult by far to be open to the presence of God when we see dog droppings, a crumpled beer can, or a polystyrene chip carton fouling the pavement. When we are confronted with the lack of reverence with which people sometimes treat our mother earth; when we are exposed to the carelessness and indifference of those who litter; when we feel helpless before the power of those who rape the earth for personal profit, it is difficult to see the face of God: "he had no form or comeliness that we should look at him, and no beauty that we should desire him. He was despised and rejected by men; a man of sorrows and acquainted with grief, and as one from whom men hide their faces he was despised, and we esteemed him not." (Is. 53: 2ff)

Equally, it is difficult to trust in the presence of a God Who, at times, seems to abandon us in moments of extreme distress. The loss of a loved one to cancer; the betrayal of marriage promises through infidelity; the loss of a job; the struggle to remain sober when addicted to drugs or alcohol; the unfairness and cruelty of life; gratuitous violence; all militate against an understanding of a God Who gazes fondly upon His children. Trust is effective only against the background of temptations to abandon it. Its light shines through the clouds of confusion and despair. Elie Wiesel, a Nobel Peace laureate and a survivor of Auschwitz, in his little book, *Night,* records

> The SS hanged two Jewish men and a youth in front of the whole camp. The men died quickly, but the death throes of the youth lasted for half an hour. "Where is God? Where is he?" someone asked behind me. As the youth still hung in torment in the noose after a long time, I heard the man call again, Where is God now?" And I heard a voice in myself answer: "Where is he? He is here. He is hanging there on the gallows" [13]

The God we worship is Emmanuel, the God with us in each and every life event, the God Who holds us silently in our grief, the God Who bears our sorrows and stands with us in solidarity with our suffering. What is crucial to hold onto in times of deep mourning and distress is that no tear goes unnoticed, no pain is without meaning. All suffering has power to redeem, to make whole. Our suffering, because we are involved in humankind, because we are members of the Body of Christ, touches the whole earth, reaches out and heals the universe because, as we suffer, we share in the sufferings

---

[13] E.Wiesel, *Night,* cited in J. Moltmann, *The Crucified God,* second edition, {London: Harper and Row, 1973) 273.

of Christ the Redeemer. In our sufferings, we heal the cosmos. Such is our dignity; such is our calling.

3. Trust in the efficacy of prayer

Trust, to paraphrase the letter to the Hebrews, is the substance of things hoped for. Trust places us in the domain of the unfulfilled, the incomplete; trust directs our thoughts and actions into the realm of the not-yet, into the future, which is yet to come. Trust possesses within itself the power to move mountains, the power to bring healing, the power to touch the lives of all humankind. Trust creates a reality beyond all understanding. When we place into the hands of the living God those who have asked us to pray for them or those about whom we are deeply concerned, a triangle of love, of compassion, is created. They are already under the gaze of God, and when we offer them to God in prayer, we connect at three intersections: We and the person prayed for at one intersection; we and God at the second intersection; and thirdly, God and the person we pray for, and so a triangle of love is formed, a reflection, if you will, of the heart of the Trinity.

The incredible beauty of this dynamic is that it continues after the period of prayer is ended. The person we pray for (let's call her Pamela to make it a little more personal) is constantly under the gaze of God; our prayer for Pamela continues to resonate in the heart of God long after we emerge from formal prayer. The reason for this is that our prayer impacts on the eternal (because God is infinite), and so Pamela not only rests under the gaze of God, but she - and whatever troubles her- is constantly brought to the mind of God, Who always responds to her with love. Not, as we well know, in the way that we hope for, but always in a way which leads to a deepening relationship with Him. Say, for example, that Pamela's sister was diagnosed with cancer. We pray for her sister, and we pray that Pamela will be comforted in her worry and anxiety. Unfortunately, the cancer is terminal, and her sister dies. Had God answered our prayer? Seemingly not. But we trust that prayer is always effective; it works in ways beyond our understanding. Otherwise, there would be no point to trust.

This is prayer focused on someone we know, someone close to us. However, prayer is both universal and infinite. What happens when we go to pray is that we are grounded in the earth and act as lightening rods for the Spirit of God. What I mean by this is that we may feel that our time of prayer has been barren and fruitless, but what happens is that the measure to which we open ourselves up to the divine presence, that presence moves in us and through us into the soil of the earth and from there reaches up and touches countless souls on the other side of the globe. It is a fantasy of mine that when I reach heaven, many a person, Indian, Belgian, Chinese, whatever, will come up and express gratitude for the time I spent in prayer on a miserable autumn day because my openness to God allowed Him to work in me and through me to touch their lives. Prayer, in effect, is an entirely selfless act.

A friend of mine, a member of the Kentucky Dominican Congregation, gave me a present when I left the United States. It was a sampler she had embroidered, and on it were the words: "To stand wordlessly, quietly, and at times darkly before God day after day changes the way we touch the earth as well as others." Not only do we touch the earth, but we touch all on the earth, and we touch all the people of the planet. Such is the power of prayer; such is our dignity and responsibility as we stand before God.

4. Mistrust of feelings

The opposite side of the coin to trust is mistrust. Earlier, we saw with the experience of the woman who encountered a bag lady at the bus stop that it is sometimes advisable to mistrust the provenance of thoughts, feelings and impulses on the assumption that always to act on feelings is impulsive and may lead to consequences far from the mind of God. One of the more insidious obstacles to growth into union with God is reliance upon feelings. There is an abiding temptation to equate closeness with God with feelings of contentment and peace and to equate distance from God with feelings of dryness and restlessness. Many people in the early stages of contemplative prayer identify feelings of warmth and peace with indications of the presence of God and interpret these feelings as signs that God looks upon them favourably. On the other hand, when they experience dryness and restlessness, they associate these feelings with the absence of God.

One of the more important lessons to learn about growth and development in the spiritual life is that feelings are to be discounted; they are not a barometer of God's closeness. Otherwise, God is always close to those who call on His name: "But Zion said, 'The Lord has forsaken me, my Lord has forgotten me. Can a woman forget her sucking child, that she should have no compassion for the son of her womb? Even these may forget, yet I will not forget you. Behold, I have graven you on the palms of my hands." (Is. 49:14-16).

In passing, it may be worth noting that the image Isaiah employs for the relationship between God and the human spirit is that of the nursing mother and the sucking child, an image which draws us, once more, into the awareness that our journey into the mystery of the Divine is a journey towards recapturing a state of being and a relationship we enjoyed at our mother's breast.

A focus on feelings is, not to put too fine a point on it, a focus on self rather than on God; it is a countermovement to *metanoia*, a turning of the mind and heart away from the Lord towards the self, and in turning away from God towards the self, one loses contact with the Divine. A few years ago, I gave a parish retreat in the Lake District in the west of England. In the middle of the retreat, I was invited to celebrate mass in the village junior school. I vested in the assembly hall and waited for the children to be ushered in. The children came in, beginning with the first class, who sat cross-legged in rows at the front. They regarded this strange priest with wide-eyed interest and open-mouthed curiosity. One by one, the teachers ushered in the classes. A class of nine-year-olds was brought in and one of the boys began to poke and prod the boy who sat next to him, making a general nuisance of himself. The teacher caught sight of the disturbance and cleared her throat loudly to get the boy's attention. When she did so, she pointed to her eyes with two fingers, turned her hand and pointed the fingers towards the altar. What she was saying, in effect, was "Eyes front" and her gesture achieved the desired result. As a parable in action, it was very effective. What her intervention said to me was that, in prayer, we need always to have our eyes directed towards the front, towards God and away from the many distractions which claim our attention.

Progress in the spiritual life is slow because we easily get distracted, but there again, it was never meant to be rapid. There are always flowers growing beside the path which leads into the kingdom of our Father and they can cause us to stop along the way in order to inhale their fragrance. This is perfectly reasonable, as long as we remember first to thank

God for the beauty and sweet aroma of creation and then to return to the path and continue the journey.

Ah, yes. But what about Ignatius's teaching on consolation and desolation in his Spiritual Exercises? Surely God gives feelings of peace and contentment when we are on the right path and feelings of desolation and darkness when we have gone astray? It would be nice to think so, but if we go back to the Gospel, we find the principle upon which Ignatius bases his rules of discernment: "Beware of false prophets, who come to you in sheep's clothing but inwardly are ravenous wolves. You will know them by their fruits. Are grapes gathered from thorns, or figs from thistles?" (Mt. 7:15-16). This is the third rule in Ignatius's Rules for perceiving and knowing the different movements in the soul which states "I call consolation every increase of hope, faith and charity, and all interior joy which calls and attracts to heavenly things and to the salvation of one's soul. And the fourth rule "I call desolation ... darkness of soul ... movement to things low and earthly ... moving to want of confidence, without hope, without love, when one finds oneself all lazy, tepid, sad, and as if separated from his Creator and Lord."[14] Toner cites a letter Ignatius wrote to students who felt that their studies distracted them from focus on God, with the result that they found themselves largely deprived of feelings of consolation. Toner writes, "Ignatius distinguishes consolation from acts of charity, humility, obedience, and the like. He assures the students that, if these acts are taken care of, they need have little concern about how much consolation God gives. *The latter is relatively unimportant*" (italics added)[15] What Ignatius is saying, effectively, is that the students should seek first the Kingdom, and everything else will be added unto them. Just as the teacher in the village school pointed to the front, so we, too, if we are to progress in prayer, must keep our eyes fixed on the face of God and not let considerations of consolation or desolation distract us. Feelings which surface in prayer are not dependable criteria for judging how we stand before God.

The reason for this is more physical than spiritual; it has largely to do with electrochemical impulses which affect the

---

[14] Ignatius of Loyola, *Exercitia Spiritualis* (Rome, 1969), rules 3 and 4.
[15] *Commentary on Saint Ignatius' Rules for the Discernment of Spirits: A Guide in the Principles and Practice*, (St Louis: The Institute of Jesuit Sources, 1982) 288.

way we feel. Ignatius gives a description of consolation which a more contemporary interpretation of the phenomenon would base its conclusions on brain activity during meditation. Andrew Newburg and associates, in one study, uncovered evidence

> that the mystical experiences of our subjects, the altered states of mind they described as the absorption of the self into something larger, were not the result of emotional mistakes or simple wishful-thinking, but were associated instead with a series of observable neurological events, which, while unusual, are not outside the range of normal brain function. In other words, mystical experience is biologically, observably, and scientifically real.[16]

Brain imaging studies indicate that different kinds of religious experience emanate from different parts of the brain. Jeeves and Brown note that

> changes in brain activity ... are not unique to a religious experience. However, the mind may certainly interpret the activity in these more general neural systems as a kind of religious state, colored by the religious context of the experience and the personal history of the individual.[17]

Ignatius describes desolation in his fourth rule as "darkness of soul ... movement to things low and earthly ... moving to want of confidence, without hope, without love,

---

[16] A. Newburg, et al. *Why God Wont Go Away: Brain Science and the Biology of Belief,* (New York: Ballantine Books, 2002) 7.

[17] M. Jeeves and W. S. Brown, *Neuroscience Psychology and Religion: Illusions, Delusions, and Realities about Human Nature* (West Conshohocken, Pennsylvania: Templeton Foundation Press, 2009) 99.

when one finds oneself all lazy, tepid, sad."[18] The American Psychiatric Association's Diagnostic and Statistical Manual of Mental Disorders lists feelings of sadness or emptiness, feelings of restlessness, agitation, fatigue and loss of energy as symptoms indicating depression; they have little to do with our relationship with God. What Ignatius calls desolation may well be a mood disorder, the aetiology of which is complex, embracing physiological, psychological, environmental and hereditary factors.

Without diminishing the importance of the various factors which contribute to the development of a depressive episode, one factor has relevance to the main thrust of this book, namely, the effects of inadequate child-rearing practices. John Bowlby, in his work on attachment theory in the 1960s, proposed that there is a correlation between the emergence of depression in adulthood with the weakness of the bond between baby and mother during infancy. Say, for instance, the baby is unwanted; the mother suffers from post-partum depression; there is poor emotional connection between mother and baby; or most tragically of all, the mother dies in childbirth. All these

---

[18] Toner, *Commentary on Saint Ignatius*, 288.

factors have a harmful effect upon the baby's formation of self-concept. Experience of loss, experience of not being held, as we saw in the work of René Spitz, experience of being rejected by the one we depend on for survival all contribute to a self-understanding which is impoverished and warped. The child grows to adulthood feeling unwanted and unloved and projects these feelings onto God in prayer.

The metaphor often used for depression is that of cloud. We speak of a cloud of despair, a cloud of confusion, a darkness of spirit. In a different sense, it is the metaphor by which the anonymous author in the fourteenth century denotes the distance which separates us from God (the cloud of unknowing) and the receptacle into which we are called to jettison all the cares and attachments which impede our spiritual growth (the cloud of forgetting):

> We are apt to think that we are very far from God because of this cloud of unknowing between us and him, but surely it would be more correct to say that we are much farther from him if there is no cloud of forgetting between us and the whole created world.... In a word, everything must be hidden under the cloud of forgetting.[19]

---

[19] *The Cloud of Unknowing,* (Harmondsworth, Middlesex: Penguin Books,1981), Chapter 5, 66,67.

The cloud of unknowing, which stands between us and God, again is no indication of the distance or closeness of God to the human heart; the cloud is a constant presence, and it is only by entering into the cloud, as Moses did, that we can come face to face with the living God. Feelings basically are a distraction and if we focus on them, we give them power to which they are not entitled.

There are two things to consider here: the first is that if we hanker after feelings of peace in time of prayer, or outside prayer, for that matter, then we are going to prayer with the intention of getting something out of it. In other words, we are acting from selfish motives. Secondly, a desire for consolation in prayer is, in itself, a marker for how little we have progressed on the spiritual journey. We are babes, in the sense referred to by Paul in his first letter to Corinthians: "But I, brethren, could not address you as spiritual men, but as men of the flesh, as babes in Christ. I fed you with milk, not solid food; for you were not ready for it; and even yet you are not ready, for you are still of the flesh" (1 Cor. 3:1-3a). There is a world of difference between being babes of the flesh and babes of the spirit.

What I have attempted to do in this chapter is to map out some of the territory of spiritual development. The main focus has been on trust as the first developmental gain of infancy; trust was seen firstly as trust in the process. The process involves four movements: from activity to passivity; from the impersonal to the personal; from insensitivity to the work of the Spirit towards a heightened sensitivity to the Spirit's movements; and from a need to control towards a surrender of self. The second focus of trust is that of trust in the abiding presence of God. The third focus is trust in the efficacy of prayer, and finally, these three expressions of trust are balanced with a healthy mistrust, and the focus of mistrust is on a too-ready identification of feelings as a barometer of our standing with God.

As the first chapter's perspective is on trust as the wellspring of connectedness the perspective adopted in chapter 2 will be on hope as the force which allows us to view spiritual growth and development within the context of the culture and social pressures in which we live, move, and have our being.

Chapter 2

Second Perspective:
Hope: Light Shining in Darkness

But the faith and the love and the hope are all in the waiting.
Wait without thought, for you are not ready for thought;
So the darkness shall be the light, and the stillness the dancing.
T.S. Eliot, "East Coker"[1]

I begin this second chapter in the same way I began chapter 1, that is, with a journey in time and memory to an event which touched me very deeply. On that occasion, I attended a charismatic healing service in Bradford. The service was conducted by an American priest who was noted for his gift of healing. There were a number of people in wheelchairs in the sanctuary and I noticed a young woman who was about eighteen or nineteen. What was striking about her besides her attractiveness was her look of intense longing and anticipation. She yearned with a desire beyond words to be healed of her affliction. The ache in her heart was such that it burned an

---

[1] T.S. Eliot, "East Coker" in *Four Quartets* (London: Faber & Faber, 1979) 2-4.

image into my memory, to the extent that it remains as vivid today as it did all those years ago.

That young woman is a living example of what Paul writes about in his letter to the Romans: "we ourselves who have the first fruits of the Spirit, groan inwardly as we wait [for] ... the redemption of our bodies. For in this hope we were saved. Now hope that is seen is not hope. For who hopes for what he sees? But if we hope for what we do not see, we wait for it with patience." (Rm. 8:23-25). And therein lies the rub. The journey into the mystery of the Divine is marked by patient waiting in order to allow God's plan to unfold in our hearts. The waiting is an Advent prayer, not confined to its own proper season before Christmas, but the prayer of waiting which lies at the core of what it means to be human, resting silently, darkly, in the very depths of the soul. We shall return to this theme in chapter 5.

There are special qualities attached to this Advent prayer, one of which is an expectation informed by that sense of longing or yearning seen on the face of the young woman in Bradford all those years ago. The psalmist beautifully expresses the longing of the human heart: "I wait for the Lord, my soul waits, in his word I hope; my soul waits for the Lord more than watchmen for the morning, more than watchmen for morning" (Ps. 30: 5f.). And again in Psalm 84: "My soul longs, yea, faints for the courts of the Lord." This is the longing deep within the human heart which stands patiently before the God of our tomorrows, a longing that He may bring fulfilment to the promise.

What is even more significant is the fact that the longing of the human heart creates a void, an empty space for the divine creative activity to take place. However, accepting the void goes against the grain because nature abhors a vacuum and the temptation is to fill the emptiness of waiting, much as Peter did when told to wait for the Lord in Galilee. Peter, uncomfortable with waiting decided to go fishing and he and his companions fished all night and caught nothing (Jn. 21), signifying the futility of relying on human resources alone. Even in human terms, one of the signs of maturity is the ability to defer gratification. Children demand instant satisfaction; adults are able (at least sometimes) to resist the temptation to run to the refrigerator each time they feel a little peckish. The Advent prayer demands that we wait patiently for the coming of the Lord in an attitude of complete surrender, before the unfolding of the mystery of the Divine.

In the previous chapter we reflected on the nature of trust; here we shall look at our relationship with God from the perspective of hope, whilst not forgetting the intimate connection between hope and trust. In his essay on hope, Rudolph Bultmann[2] writes that trust is one of three elements which constitute hope. The other two are expectation of the future and patient waiting. This chapter is about hope, not so much as a theological virtue, but as that attribute of human nature which, in one of its manifestations, forms the ground upon which trust is built, trust which is the basic orientation we bring to prayer and which is at the root of a deepening relationship with God. It expresses the conviction that "For God alone, my soul waits in silence; from him comes my salvation" (Ps. 62:1).

In the letter to the Hebrews, we read that trust is the substance of hope (Heb. 11:1) and trust, directed as it is towards the fulfilment of the Promise draws us into the

---

[2] R. Bultmann, *"The Early Christian Concept of Hope"* In Theological Dictionary of the New Testament, vol. II, Ed. Gerhard Kittel, Trans. Geoffrey W. Bromley,(Grand Rapids, Michigan: Wm. B. Eerdmans) 1964, 531ff.

domain of the "not-yet." As we saw earlier, the delicate dance of development is a circular movement, bringing us back to the place where we started, back to the time when, as infants, we faced our first psychosocial crisis, that of resolving the tension between trust and mistrust. Truth be told, the tension is never fully resolved; the dance still goes on.

It is important to realise that from the very start of life, hope enters the scene and plays a crucial role in resolving the first developmental crisis. Successful resolution of the crisis depends on the presence of the hope that needs will be met. The basic orientation of the baby is that of hope: hope that the mother will provide food, warmth and physical contact, and when she does, the baby can begin to rely on the dependability of the environment. Erikson regards hope as the first and most fundamental of the "vital virtues" possessed by human beings. He describes these virtues as "certain qualities which begin to animate man pervasively during successive stages of his life."[3] For Erikson, hope is "the most essential overall

---

[3] E. H. Erikson, *Identity, Youth and Crisis* (New York and London: W.W. Norton & Co. 1968) 233.

outlook on life."[4] But there is more to hope than that. John McQuarrie asks, "Is it a passion, a biological mechanism, a theological virtue?"[5] While agreeing with McQuarrie that hope is "a disposition of the whole person"[6] I would venture to suggest that hope is sufficiently expansive to incorporate all the meanings he attributes to hope.

But first, we need to set the context in which the elements of hope may be explored. Spiritual development doesn't exist in a vacuum but emerges against the backdrop of those life situations in which we find ourselves: genetic, environmental, historical. We are products of a complex mix of factors which have helped to shape our personality and character, and so it is that hope unfolds as a response to those factors, both personal and environmental, which elicit such a response. The dynamics of hope, as we shall see, emerge from two sources: (i) external, that is, born of personal, social, economic and political events which impact upon our lives from the outside, and (ii) internal, that is, arising from the longings of the human heart which

---

[4] E. H. Erikson and H. Q. Kivnick, *Vital Involvement in Old Age* (New York and London: W. W. Norton & Co. 1989) 33.
[5] J. McQuarrie, *Christian Hope* (S.C.M. Press Ltd., 1978) 103.
[6] *Ibid.*

no amount of self-soothing can assuage. In the external realm, hope invariably springs from a situation of conflict, whether conflict is experienced on a personal, social, or religious level. The precise nature of this conflict resides in the opposition between immanence and transcendence: between the here-and-now and the not-yet, between present and future, between the human and the divine.

More concretely, hope emerges in the interface between a critical event or series of events and the response to those events. This response is expressed as a conviction that this state of affairs must not be allowed to dominate but must be resisted. For instance, the young woman mentioned above was confined in a wheelchair; she desired with all her heart to change her condition. Like the woman with an issue of blood in the Gospel, she had presumably tried all means at her disposal to find a cure. Resorting to human means did not alleviate the suffering of the young woman in Bradford, so she placed her trust and confidence in God Who alone could cure her. Her presence at the healing service was an external expression of the hope she felt. Had she not been handicapped she would have had no reason to hope, at least not with such a degree of intensity or specificity. Her hope arose from her condition and her profound need to have God alter that condition. Secondly, and of equal significance, her hope was grounded in her bodily frailty and arose precisely and exclusively from her physical condition.

The conclusion we can draw from this observation is that the genesis of hope, from the internal perspective, is built into the human organism and arises from deep within the human condition. Consequently, hope, understood in human terms, always emerges from a concrete, physical situation and is embedded in human nature in its basic orientation to be ever open to future possibility. Therefore, hope is both material and spiritual and by virtue of its dual reality, hope collapses the age-old dichotomy between spirit and flesh, encouraging a holistic, non-divisive approach to spiritual development. Such an approach demands that we discard (or at least place in abeyance) traditional models of hope and traditional language by which reflections on the nature of hope are articulated and embrace an understanding and a language more reflective of our times. Sallie McFague notes,

Language that supports hierarchical, dualistic, external, unchanging, atomistic, anthropocentric, and deterministic ways of understanding [the relationship between God and the world and between ourselves and the world] is not appropriate *for our time,* whatever its appropriateness might have been for other times. It would appear that the appropriate language for our time, in the sense of being true to the paradigm of reality in which we actually live, would support ways of understanding the God-world, and human-world relationships as open, caring, inclusive, interdependent, changing, mutual, and creative.[7]

To adopt the approach which McFague advocates will demand a break from traditional ways of thinking; it will demand, in effect, a radical conversion experience in order to embrace the "new thing" of which Isaiah writes (Is. 43: 19), namely, the in-breaking of the God of promise. Conversion involves a letting go of previous paradigms which tend to be static and inflexible, such as the flesh-spirit paradigm. Running through the history of Western thought is an assumption, as mentioned earlier, that there is a divide between body and spirit where the body, consisting of matter, is thought to be imperfect and prone to illness and decay, and the spirit, being incorporeal, is thought to be untainted by the flesh.

---

[7] S. McFague, *Models of God: Theology for an Ecological, Nuclear Age* (Philadelphia: Fortress Press, 1987) 13.

I imagine that many people who have an interest in spiritual development regard such development as something which exclusively concerns the spirit in isolation from concerns of a material nature, such as social, cultural and environmental issues. In other words, spiritual growth and development is often understood as being exclusively devoted to nonmaterial as opposed to physical or material concerns. According to this way of thinking, hope would be interpreted as a theological virtue, as an abstraction, as a state of mind rather than as a biological mechanism which promotes physical, social, and psychological development as well as spiritual development when directed towards God. The main thrust of the argument in this chapter is that hope, at least in its external grounding, arises from concrete physical experiences embedded in the day-to-day world in which we live. And it is precisely in the experience of conflict that hope emerges as a response.

When I was a student in Paris in the sixties, we used to have a crusty old abbé to lunch on Sundays. One Sunday, at table, we were discussing the recent changes in the liturgy arising out of the second Vatican Council. The abbé became more and more agitated until, finally, he slammed down his knife and fork and loudly exclaimed, "Je ne bouge plus!" (I'm not moving any further). This is, I suppose, one way to respond to change, but not necessarily conducive to growth. Another response to a critical situation is to try to resolve it by using natural means. The problem with this approach is that natural means are usually insufficient to resolve the crisis.

Way back in the eighth century BCE, between the years 735 and 733 BCE a crisis arose in Judah, described in 2 Kings 16:5-9. Ahaz came to the throne of Judah when he was twenty (see 2 Kings 16:2) and immediately found his throne and the whole country under threat of invasion from three directions, from the north by the Aramean-Israelite coalition, from the south by the Edomites, who had succeeded in driving Ahaz's troops from Elath and from the west by the Philistines, who had made incursions into the Negev.[8] What does he do? He throws money (not his own) at it. He raids the temple treasury to send lavish gifts to the king of Assyria in order to persuade him to come to his aid. Isaiah confronted Ahaz on the road

---

[8] For the historical background, cf. J. Bright, *A History of Israel,* Second
    Edition, (London: SCM Press, 1972) 267ff.

to the Fuller's Field. as the king attempted to safeguard the water supply for Jerusalem (see Is.7: 1ff). Seen in this context, the prophet's injunction, "Take heed, be quiet, do not fear and do not let your heart be faint" (Is.7:4) is unrealistic, even bordering on the foolhardy. An impassioned plea to trust in God's promise carries slender weight when placed against a threat of imminent attack.

In the light of subsequent events, however, the prophet showed great wisdom and insight. Why deplete the temple treasury to bribe Tiglath-Pileser to pursue a course of action he intended to follow anyway? In 733 BCE the Assyrian king invaded Galilee and deported large sections of the population (2K. 15:19), thus averting the threat posed by the Aramean-Israelite coalition by annexing great swathes of territory for himself.

Hope, then, emerges from a dynamic process: On the one hand, there is the critical event -be it personal, national or global - and, on the other, there is the willingness to take a critically negative stance against what Shakespeare calls "the slings and arrows of outrageous fortune." Hope springs from actual encounter with the reality of our everyday world, not primarily from the desires of the human spirit and it is grounded, at least in a spiritual context, in an abiding commitment to the proposition that God is the God of Promise and that, in God's good time, He will bring the Promise to fulfilment. Hope takes us out of the warm cosy world of the inside and exposes us to the chill winds of the outside. And this adds a whole new dimension to spiritual development because it exposes us to the real world rather than insulates us in a private world of contemplation, protected from the intrusions of external reality.

This, then, is a chapter about hope, not hope as dreams, vague aspirations or wishful thinking, but about that quality of human life essential to the well-being of women and men as they live their lives against a backdrop of a variety of crises on a personal and global level. Spiritual development, I repeat, does not occur in a vacuum but is shaped not only by divine activity but also, on a human level, by genetics and cultural, social, historical, political and economic influences which affect our lives. These influences exert their hold universally, whether one is a working mother or an enclosed nun; no one can escape because spiritual development is shaped by social and cultural forces as well as the prompting of the Spirit. Not that we can separate the activity of the Spirit from external influences, for it is precisely within those external influences that the Spirit works. The Word is becoming flesh in the realities of our daily lives. The journey into the mystery of the Divine, then, calls us to engage with the world in which we live, with all its beauty and wonder but also with all its blindness, self-serving arrogance and pride. Spiritual development encompasses the whole of human experience and is not restricted to formal prayer and acts of devotion but demands an involvement with the whole of created reality.

The pain of the world accompanies us along our journey, both in its global manifestation as well as our own personal experience of doubt, grief, heartache and powerlessness. We move along a path frequently marked by personal tragedy, where sorrow clouds the heart. At the personal level, we have to contend with times of failure; times of grief; times of loneliness; times of being misunderstood and taken for granted; times of rejection; times of loss; times of illness; times of dying. We live our lives against a backdrop of various crises: war; international terrorism; global warming; drought;

famine; starvation; overpopulation; pollution of rivers and seas; deforestation; declining natural resources; economic collapse. All these crises take their toll, as we attempt to engage in the process of spiritual growth towards maturity. This chapter explores various elements of hope, viewed as a dialectic process under the following headings: A. Hope as a response to crisis; B. Hope as impetus towards conversion; C. Hope as ground of human becoming; D. Hope as passion-fire.

A. Hope as a Response to Crisis

One of the central themes in a contemporary philosophy of history is crisis. "The modern consciousness of history is a consciousness of crisis and all modern philosophy of history is, in the last analysis, a philosophy of crisis."[9] Modern social consciousness came to birth in the cultural earthquake of the French Revolution, one of the most cataclysmic events in Europe in the late eighteenth century. The French Revolution brought in its train a radically different orientation to reality and a fundamentally different change in perspective from which reality was to be viewed. The breakdown in social,

---

[9]   J. Moltmann, *Theology of Hope*, (London and New York: SCM Press, 1967) 230.

political and ecclesiastic structures presented a profound challenge to human self-understanding and to the easy assumptions people previously made. Exposure to the breakdown of institutions and social structures hitherto taken for granted occasioned feelings of insecurity and uncertainty before the future. The lack of assurance, coupled with the explosive violence which brought these changes to pass, brought to human awareness the ever-present and all-pervasive phenomenon of crisis, and crisis is, as I contend, one of the catalysts of hope.

With the French Revolution, a new consciousness came to birth. This event violently ruptured the entire world view of late eighteenth-century Europeans. It was a watershed in which the prevailing interpretation of reality was challenged and rejected, where the power and control exercised by institutions, both church and state, collapsed and where human beings were liberated from the oppressive determinism of class structure (or, at least, were opened to the possibility of change). Immanuel Kant, whose work, *Der Streit der Fakultäten* (Conflict of the Faculties) was published in the year of the Revolution, writes, "A phenomenon of this kind can never again be forgotten because it has disclosed in human nature a predisposition and capacity for improvement, such as no politician could have thought up on the basis of the course of things so far."[10] The unimaginable, the unforeseen, the unthinkable were arising in human consciousness and people began to inhabit a world which was no longer the exclusive domain of those in power. One might well interpret these events, for all their destructiveness and violence, as signs of the in-breaking of the Kingdom of God, which proclaims liberty to captives: "Do not think that I have come to bring peace on earth; I have not come to bring peace, but a sword" (Mt. 10:34). There came into being, as a direct result of the Revolution, "an awareness of the totally historic character of life as the total criticalness of man's world."[11] The world of human beings had become critical for a variety of reasons and from a variety of different standpoints, and the critical stance taken against the constructs of society engendered a consciousness of freedom, of new and exciting possibilities. Hegel writes of a "glorious

---

[10] I. Kant, *Der Streit der Fakultäten,* In Gesammelte Schriften, vol. 7, 1917, 79, cited in Moltmann, *Theology of Hope,* 231 footnote.
[11] *Ibid.*

dawn," and Fichte describes his doctrine of science as "the first system of freedom."[12]

The price, however, which one has to pay for this freedom is the anxiety provoked by the uncertainty before a world in a constant state of movement and unrest. Human beings had to construct for themselves a world which is intelligible and stable and relate to that world against a backdrop of permanent crisis; they had, and still have, to cope with the stress, the discomfort, and the uncertainty which such a state of affairs occasions. Not only is the state of crisis permanent, but it is also all-embracing. No area of human experience or human endeavour lies outside its influence. "Can I keep up my mortgage payments if I lose my job?" "Do the elderly have to choose between eating and staying warm?" "Into what sort of world are my children growing up, and how can I protect them from the pernicious intrusions of porn on the internet?" "Have we already passed the point of no-return with regard to global warming?" "How will the hungry be fed?" "Where is God in all this?" These are distressing questions; they are all

---

[12] *Ibid.*

depressing thoughts, except for the presence of the beauty and luminance of hope.

The French Revolution provides but one illustration of a world in crisis and a radical shift in emphasis away from the past towards the future. The same dynamic is at play in the preaching of the prophets in the Old Testament. The same elements of crisis and the critical stance taken against futile attempts to resolve the crisis from within are present. The prophetic voice proclaims the will of God within a concrete situation of crisis. In each case, it is the immediacy of threat which impels the prophet to stand against received wisdom and accepted ways of responding to the threat. The prophet adopts a stance of critical negativity (a phrase coined by the German philosopher Theodor W. Adorno) against political expediency, which relies on human resources rather than placing trust in God. The prophetic call is a call to hope, trusting in the promises which God has made to Israel. Even a cursory reading of the prophetic literature brings to awareness a pattern common to each individual prophet: faced with a concrete social or political crisis, the ruling class responds in exclusively political or military ways. The prophet stands against these attempts, pointing to the incongruity of a nation, which is God's possession, taking its destiny into its own hands. The prophet points to trusting hope in God's protection as the only authentic way forward: "Assyria shall not save us. We will not ride upon horses; as we will say no more 'Our God' to the work of our own hands." (Hos. 14:4).

Embedded in the consciousness of the OT prophets was the conviction that crisis was the foundation experience which led to the emergence of Israel as a theocracy. The period of the Judges which was later to develop into the Assembly of Yahweh, and later still, to develop into sophisticated liturgical forms and procedures, had, as its origin a call to arms to defend the tribes against impending attack. Israel was a loose confederation of tribes; when threatened by the Philistines, heralds would be sent out to gather the tribes together for mutual defence and support. The God of Israel is the God of the Promise, and based on historical experiences, Israel came to understand itself as a chosen people, and this consciousness of election was characterised by hope that, as God had intervened and saved His people in the past, He would continue to do so in the future.

At a deeper level of consciousness lies the prophetic word. Prophetic hope stands against any attempt to resolve crises from within the parameters of human striving or by relying on traditional means of bringing a crisis to a successful resolution, as we saw from the confrontation between Isaiah and Ahaz on the road to the Fuller's Field. The prophets adopt a highly critical stance against crisis resolution from a position of immanence and focus on the transcendence of the God Who saves His people. The prophets adopted a position of critical negativity against traditional ways of responding to a crisis because those ways were largely responsible for the crisis in the first place. Precisely because traditional structures were responsible for the crisis, they cannot be relied on to resolve the crisis. "Every crisis throws up the question of the historic future. For when the whole existing situation is in a state of crisis, it becomes obvious that the future can no longer arise automatically out of the past, it can no longer be the natural repetition and continuation of the past, but that something new must be found in it."[13] "Remember, nor consider the things of old. Behold I am doing a new thing; now it springs forth" (Is.

---

[13]   J. Moltmann, *Theology of Hope* 233.

43:19). "For behold, I create new heavens and a new earth; and the former things shall not be remembered or come to mind" (Is. 65:17). The "new thing" accomplished by God is the divine light, which illuminates and fires the prophetic vision. There is a profound insight as well as a stark challenge contained within the prophetic vision. The prophet orientates himself towards that which is possible rather than towards the actual and this carries him far beyond the realm of human endeavour into the sphere of divine transcendence, the sphere in which hope becomes active.

This orientation offers a lesson to the one embarked on a journey of spiritual development, a lesson which demands a radical, unequivocal and uncompromising response to the invitation to allow oneself to be drawn out of the need for assurance and certainty into self-forgetting and self-surrender in encounter with the Divine. The journey of hope is a journey into the Cloud of Unknowing, precisely because the future is unknown and the fact that God, by virtue of His boundlessness, is also essentially unknown.

Further, the prophet orientates himself towards the transcendent out of a conviction that he is dominated by God:

"For the Lord spoke thus to me with his strong hand upon me, and warned me not to walk in the way of this people." (Is.8:11). The way of this people is a way of reliance upon human resources rather than upon God; it is a way which has been subjected to critical judgement and found to be sadly lacking. "There is the uncompromising insistence on reserving the initiative to God alone. All human activity is ruled out and human beings are to remain passive in the face of the Godhead."[14]

Here, we are confronted with one of the major difficulties which impedes spiritual development, namely, the reluctance to place one's hope in God alone and to remain passive before His face. "Cast your burden on the Lord and he will sustain you" (Ps. 55: 22) is the counsel of the Psalmist. However, we look to the One who did precisely that and see that "in the days of his flesh, Jesus offered up prayers and supplications, with loud cries and tears, to him who was able to save him from death" (Heb. 5:7), and yet he was not spared. There is more than a sneaking suspicion that, were we to jettison human prudence and hope in God alone, then a similar fate would befall us. We

---

[14] *Ibid.*

are confronted with the self-emptying of the Son before the Father and are terrified, albeit subconsciously, of the cost that such self-gift entails. Such self-giving defies all reason, and let's face it, we are reasonable human beings.

Hope as Thrust towards Conversion.

In the introduction, I quoted Gustavo Gutierrez's description of conversion as "a permanent process in which very often the obstacles we meet make us lose all we had gained and start anew."[15] What is relevant here are the sentences which follow: "The fruitfulness of our conversion depends on our openness to doing this, *our spiritual childhood*. All conversion implies a break. To wish to accomplish it without conflict is to deceive ourselves and others" [16] Here, once more, we are confronted with the paradox where the conversion process orientates us towards the future on the one hand and, on the other, calls for a return to what Gutierrez describes as an embrace of "our spiritual childhood." Within the core dynamics of the conversion process into which hope immerses us, lie two separate but interlocking movements: a

---

[15] G. Gutierrez, *A Theology of Liberation* (London: SCM Press, 1981) 205.
[16] *Ibid.*

letting go and a change in orientation. Firstly, let us explore more fully the process of letting go before considering the constant need to orientate ourselves towards the future.

Hope: Movement towards Self-Emptying

Perhaps I may have been a little too hasty in treating lightly traditional approaches to spiritual growth, specifically those which favour an ascetic approach based on self-discipline, upon the need, in other words, to "enter by the narrow gate … For the gate is narrow and the way is hard that leads to life, and those who find it are few" (Mt. 7:13- 14). Obviously, there is a profound truth contained in this counsel to embrace the hard way which leads to life, instead of espousing a soft option. The way into the mystery of the Divine is rarely easy or straightforward. This text reminds me of the countless times I have sat with people on their journey into life and been faced with the complaint, "But it's so hard." Of course it is. What on earth do you expect? The exhortation to enter by the narrow gate is set against a background of what Jerusalem was like in the time of Jesus. At that time, the gates of the city were closed at night and reopened at dawn. What was to happen, then, to the unfortunate soul who arrived after sunset? Provision seems to have been made for such an eventuality because beside each gate there was, apparently, a narrow slit sufficiently wide to admit a person, but not large enough to accommodate any baggage he or she might be carrying. In order to enter the city, the citizen had to divest of backpack and suitcase, remove the bird cage and bookcase, leave the donkey outside the gate, aware that it was highly likely that the donkey would be stolen before the break of dawn. Therefore, in order to tread the path of life, it is necessary to set aside all that is cumbersome; otherwise, like the rich young man, we shall walk away sad.

During the 1980s, I went to work in South Africa. Leaving England meant leaving behind much of what I had accumulated over time. It made rather a mockery of my vow of poverty, but there you are: Nobody's perfect. Anything which could not fit into the boot of the car was left behind. Gone was the collection of books I had amassed over years of study; gone were my record player and collection of records I had lovingly gathered, many of which were gifts from friends and held a special place in my heart, apart that is, from the intrinsic joy of the music itself; gone were clothes that I would no longer need; perhaps most painful of all was the loss of the company of family and friends who had been my companions through life and upon whose support I had come to rely so heavily. Literally, I was being stripped almost bare for the journey, and what made the loss bearable was the conviction that the God I worship was calling me out of my future into a bright place of promise and, above all, a place of hope.

The dynamics of hope encourage a letting go of all that impedes us from moving into the mystery of the Divine. It involves a willingness to renounce a dependence on human resources, letting go of assumptions, letting go of the past, particularly those parts of the past which we view with regret for mistakes made, for words we wish had remained unsaid; letting go of resentment; and perhaps most necessarily of all, letting go of fear. Fear is a big obstacle to engaging in the process of spiritual growth. Of what are we afraid? Financial insecurity? Our children's future? Aging and dementia? Of not measuring up to some self-imposed and unrealistic ideal? Of not making a difference? Of not being loved by God? Of retribution for our sins? In the words of the *Benedictus*, God has sworn an oath to Abraham "to grant us that we, being delivered from the hand of our enemies, might serve him without fear, in holiness and righteousness before him all the days of our life" (Lk. 1:73-75).

Perhaps, however, anxiety, rather than fear, would be a more accurate description of those negative feelings which assail us from time to time. And this is where we need to be gentle with ourselves. Anxiety is often the product of overactive chemicals in the brain and not a sign of moral weakness on our part. If we tell ourselves that we shouldn't be feeling this way, then all we are doing is compounding the problem by adding a veneer of guilt to what is already an unpleasant experience. It is tempting to think that if I had more faith, then I wouldn't feel this way. Jesus gives ample assurance, by virtue of his Gethsemane experience, that anxiety and fear are not obstacles to a relationship with God but can, in fact, act as a goad to placing ourselves, even tentatively, into the hands of the living God.

Fear is not the only obstacle to the abandonment of the self before God. A more pernicious trait is self-will. Ignatius of Loyola's prayer, *Suscipe,* is a wonderful antidote to this all-too-human tendency:

Take, Lord, and receive all my liberty, my memory, my understanding, and my entire will - all that I have and call my own. You have given it all to me. To you. Lord, I return it. Everything is yours; do with it what you will. Give me only your love and your grace. That is enough for me.[17]

Self-will may often be cloaked in trappings of piety; such was the case with St Eulalia, the co-patron of Barcelona. In 304 CE, Eulalia was a Spanish Christian girl who was confined to the house when she was thirteen, because everyone was required to pay homage to Roman gods and her mother knew that if she let Eulalia out, there would be hell to pay, as indeed there was. "She lived," according to H. V. Morton, "in that deplorable chapter in the history of martyrdom under Diocletian, when Christians committed suicide in their anxiety to become saints."[18] Eulalia escaped from her mother's clutches and, in her zeal, presented herself at the magistrate's court, where she promptly hurled insults at the emperor and the gods of Rome. The magistrate attempted to pacify her and gently asked her to moderate her tone. Whereupon, according to Prudentius, a poet of the fifth century, intensely angry

---

[17] In D. Fleming, S.J. *The Spiritual Exercises of St Ignatius*, St Louis: The Institute of Jesuit Resources, 1978, (Second Printing, 1980) 141.

[18] H. V. Morton, *A Stranger in Spain, (*London: Methuen, 1983) 146.

at being deprived of a martyr's crown, she roared with rage and spat in the magistrate's eye. As a result, she gained what she most desired: She was stripped, tortured and burnt at the stake. One may excuse her excesses due to the fact that she was a headstrong child. But a saint? She was so intent upon martyrdom that she neglected her mother's wishes and had her eyes fixed on herself and her own immature desires rather than upon the will of God. We can draw a certain measure of comfort from this because if a headstrong, self-serving, wilful child could be counted among the saints of God, then perhaps this means that we all have a chance.

Conversion, in short, is a process of self-emptying or, more accurately a process by which we allow God to empty us of all blocks and obstacles to divine love including fear, anxiety and self-will. But it must be remembered that the conversion process takes place through the prompting of hope and always under the gaze of the God of all kindliness. The process of self-emptying mirrors that of Christ Jesus who, according to Paul, in his letter to the Philippians, exhorts us "to have this mind among yourselves which is yours in Christ Jesus, who though he was in the form of God did not count equality with

God a thing to be grasped, but emptied himself, taking the form of a servant" (Phil. 2: 5-7). To the extent to which we allow ourselves to let go, we become conformed to the pattern of the self-emptying of Jesus, conscious all the time of the words of D. H. Lawrence, "It is a fearful thing to fall into the hands of the living God. But it is a much more fearful thing to fall out of them."[19]

In his letter to the Philippians, Paul writes, "Indeed I count everything as loss because of the surpassing worth of knowing Christ Jesus my Lord. For his sake I have suffered the loss of all things and count them as refuse in order that I may gain Christ" (Phil. 3:8). Mary, the pre-eminent disciple, reflects the self-emptying of her son in the words of the *Magnificat,* where she proclaims the greatness of the Lord precisely because "he has regarded the low estate of His handmaiden" (Lk. 1:48).

Consider for a moment the fact that emptiness of heart is the only ground in which the seeds of hope may take root. If our hearts are full of care, or regret, or envy, or resentment, if our hearts are filled with desire for success or acquisitiveness,

---

[19] D. H. Lawrence, *Complete Poems,* Edited by Vivian de Sola Pinto and Warren Roberts (Harmondsworth, Middlesex: Penguin Books, 1964) 699.

then we are in the same position as that of the innkeeper at Bethlehem who refused entry to Joseph and Mary because there was no room at the inn. If hearts and minds are full of whatever worries or preoccupies us, then there is no room in the inn of our hearts and God is doomed to stand at the door and knock. The Spirit of the living God, however, is active in those little losses and big losses to which we are heir. As the psalmist reminds us, "The Lord is close to the broken hearted, and saves the crushed in spirit" (Ps. 34:18).

Another way of illustrating the movement of the emptying work of God is to take the biblical metaphor of clay, shaped and fashioned by the hollowing of God. Jeremiah uses the metaphor of a clay pot to illustrate the way God empties us of all that holds us back from him. Under instruction from God, Jeremiah goes to the potter's house, where the potter fashions a vessel which "was spoiled in the potter's hand" and he uses the clay to rework "it into another vessel" (Jer. 18:14). In and of itself, clay serves no useful purpose other than in its potential to be shaped into a container. It is only when the God-potter, with consummate tenderness, places the clay of the human heart on the wheel of life and fashions the clay moistened by our tears in order that the hollow thus formed may become a vessel worthy to hold riches beyond measure. Mary's womb became the site of the Word becoming flesh precisely because it was empty. God's Spirit cannot make a home where there is no room. As with Mary, so with us.

If you think the experience of being emptied before God is distressing and painful, think again. There is another part of this process which is even more painful. Staying with the clay metaphor, there is another part of the process which is necessary: The earthenware jar has to be fired in the kiln before the process is complete. Self-emptying is insufficient on its own; it has to be accompanied by a sealing by fire, a process of purification.

The classic movements of the spiritual life have, as mentioned earlier, three stages: purification, illumination, and union, where purification is for those at the beginning of the journey into union with God. According to this approach, there is a gradual progression through distinct stages from purification, through illumination, towards union with God. However if, as I suggest, we look at spiritual development as a cyclic rather than a linear form of development, then each stage is not a distinct step on the ladder of perfection but is rather a way of being before God where each phase, like the ebb and flow of the tide and the ever-changing pattern of the seasons, repeats itself, and where each phase is constantly revisited and thereby becomes, at a deeper level, the locus of encounter with God. At times, through the events of daily life, we are exposed to the divine fire of purification; at times, our hearts are enlightened by the light of God's gaze; at times, we experience the harmony and peace of union with God. But then we get a toothache or quarrel with a neighbour and find ourselves back where we started. Our clarity of vision becomes clouded, and we get sidetracked by all-too-human concerns, and although we pay lip service to our dependence on God, there are far more pressing affairs to attend to. Our process of purification requires repeated interventions on the part of God, but we shall get there in the end, which, simply put, is the fruit of hope.

Hope: Movement from Past to Future

Because hope is here understood to be the root of the conversion process and because hope is directed towards the future, then the process of conversion involves a movement away from the past towards the future. When Jesus responded to the disciples' request to be taught how to pray (Mt. 6:9-13; Lk.11:1-13) He did so with exquisite sensitivity to the reality of the human condition as unfinished and incomplete. The structure of the Lord's Prayer is an acknowledgement of a human lack of fulfilment and a human desire for completeness; its orientation leads us away from the past towards the future, a journey which is rooted and grounded in hope.

Anchored as it is in the very heart of what it means to be human, the Lord's Prayer also confronts us with a paradigm shift of cosmic proportions. Prior to Jesus' preaching of the Kingdom, the religion of Israel was orientated largely towards the past, an orientation which ran counter to Israel's understanding of itself as children of the Promise. The God of Israel is the God of Abraham, Isaac, and Jacob, the God Who worked mighty wonders in delivering the children of Israel from slavery. Religious thought and practice were largely confined to a series of rituals and observances which were handed down from the past. Tradition, the handing down, was sometimes given precedence over the more compelling demands of justice and compassion at least according to the criticism levelled against the religious leaders in the Gospels.

This is not to say that Israel was not constantly being called to account in the preaching of the prophets. "Therefore I have hewn them by the prophets, I have slain them by the word of my mouth, and my judgement goes forth as the light. For I desire steadfast love and not sacrifice, the knowledge of God, rather than burnt offerings" (Hos. 6: 5-6).

The Lord's Prayer reveals the content of that "something new" to which Second Isaiah refers. The "something eternally new" is the invitation by God to let go of the past and embrace a future, with all its challenges and uncertainties. In his book *God, the Future of Man,* Edward Schillebeeckx writes:

> This change which has come about in man's attitude towards the world: Instead of professing his belief in the primacy of the past (and thus of tradition), he is now actively engaged in claiming primacy for the future may be called the exponent of the whole process of change.[20]

For Schillebeeckx, there is a pervasive uncertainty underlying such a change in orientation, a recognition that we are no longer secure in our assumptions and no longer masters

---

[20] E. Schillebeeckx, *God the Future of Man,* (London and Sydney: T & T Clark, 1969) 172.

of our destiny, and this, in turn, opens the door to self-doubt. In other words, the shift from past to future undermines our confidence in our own ability to shape our own ends. The implications of this change are far-reaching and all-embracing, touching every aspect of life. We do things in a certain way because we have always done them in a certain way, the way our fathers and mothers did them. Furthermore, there is no other way of doing them, or so we believe. This is a way of understanding our world, an understanding which locks us into a dogmatic, static, rigid, unimaginative, sterile way of constructing our realities and absolves us from the necessity of thinking for ourselves and using our critical faculties.

What is more distressing is that it prevents our embracing a vision of a universe into which we are constantly being invited by the living God. In other words, we lose our way. This is not to say that the past has no value. Quite the contrary. In our movement into the mystery of the Divine, one of the more reliable lamps to light our way is history and the lessons she teaches us, lessons to which we need to pay attention. George Santayana reminds us that those who cannot remember the past are condemned to repeat it. We exist in a stream of ever-unfolding, of ever-expanding evolution, and we are heirs to a whole range of insights and depths of wisdom which support and sustain us as long as we do not allow ourselves to be imprisoned in the past.

As noted above, at the end of the eighteenth century, there was a movement towards claiming the primacy of the future over the past, thus allowing for the possibility that human beings could relate differently to their world and, by extension, could relate differently to their God. Turning away from the past towards the future is an imperative which may seem to contradict the basic thrust of this book because focus on hope as an agency directed towards the future appears, at first sight, to stand against an orientation towards the past, towards that place of beginnings.

This apparent contradiction is resolved if we remember that the movement involved in spiritual growth, I suggest, is not vertical or horizontal but spherical, a movement which mirrors the movement of the planets, the rhythm of the seasons, a movement which is expansive and, under God, eternal. Our movement towards beginnings is a movement towards new beginnings. Spiritual development leads us into human becoming, and because these movements are spherical and orbital, they involve a return to the place where we started where, as Eliot would have it, we discover the place for the first time.

The prophets are true heralds of hope when the people of Israel experience national disaster, setback and exile. The God we meet in prayer is the God of Promise, a refuge for all who call on him. "Behold I will allure her and bring her into the wilderness and speak tenderly to her. And there I will … make the Valley of Achor a door of hope" (Hos. 2:14f.). Shame and disgrace followed the defeat of Israel by the men of Ai in the valley of trouble (Achor) (see Jos. chapter 7) and God's promise for Hosea is to turn everything upside down and to make trouble the very doorway of hope. Also, in Jeremiah's letter to the exiles, the Promise is not so much deliverance from present danger but the gift of hope. "When seventy years are completed for Babylon I will visit you, and I will fulfil to you my promise and bring you back to this place. For I know the plans I have for you, says the Lord, plans for welfare and not for evil, to give a future and a hope" (Jer. 29:10f).

Hope as Ground of Human Becoming

In the previous chapter, I drew attention to the consideration that we are unlike other mammals in that we lack a biologically determined relationship to the environment. Drawing on insights from evolutionary biology and developmental psychology, we see that hope, arising as it does from a situation of human conflict, may be interpreted as a reflection of a whole process of adaptation to the environment, as Erikson illustrates in the first of his developmental stages. What is crucial to remember, however, is that this process of adaptation is a response to the God under whose gaze we live, have our being, and move ever more deeply into the mystery of divine love.

The spiritual aspect of this adaptation is prophetic in that we take a critical stance against the values and assumptions of society, as did all the prophets of the OT, culminating in the stance adopted by Jesus, a stance which ultimately led to his death. Hope is not optional, an extra in the process of spiritual development, but is a force embedded in the human condition by virtue of the structure of human nature as non-specific. If I may paraphrase Robert Kegan's remark in his book *The*

Evolving Self might we not better understand ourselves in the predicaments we face, personal and global, if we could have a better understanding of how the way we live and the quality of our prayer reflect the level of our hoping, "not the hoping we have or do but the hope and hoping we are."[21] Hope, I repeat, is the genetically programmed feature of human becoming, hardwired into the evolutionary process of human openness to the world. The human organism is destined to engage in the dance of self-preservation and self-transcendence, not because we have an option, but because, paradoxically, we come to be as human beings according to the measure that we transcend ourselves. And the energy that generates the movement of self-transcendence, to move beyond the borders imposed by our own physicality, is hope.

A second consideration that gives rise to the thought that hope is a biological mechanism stems from the perception of hope as a mental operation. A human being starts out as a bodily reality, and as Winnicott maintains, out of this bodily reality the psyche emerges. All that belongs to psyche, all

---

[21] R. Kegan, *The Evolving Self: Problem and Process in Human Development,* (Cambridge, Massachusetts, and London, Harvard University Press, 1982) 4.

that pertains to psychic structure has its origin and base in a physical substratum. If this is true, then it leads one to the assumption that hope, as a mental operation, must be grounded in the soma and emerge from a body-based psyche.

If it is correct to assume that hope is grounded in a bodily base, having its origins in bodily experience, then it would be equally correct to assume that hope is implicated in the libidinal and aggressive drives which dictate so much of mental and physical activity. Hope, then, is not only a rather abstract reflection of the state of openness to the world and the drive for self-transcendence but also, more concretely, the force underlying the most primitive expressions of creativity and aggression. Winnicott offers some insight into the manner in which hope lies at the base of both libidinal and aggressive drives when he offers for our consideration the idea that hope is the energy underlying the creative and aggressive gestures first seen in the bodily movements of the tiny baby, an energy that impels each of us to reach out creatively and aggressively to establish contact and, in the present context, contact with the Divine.

Hope as Passion-Fire

To embrace and respond to the call to enter more deeply into the mystery of the Divine is an act of passion fuelled by hope. Earlier in the chapter, I quoted McQuarrie's questions: "Is it a passion, a biological mechanism, a theological virtue?" And I maintain it is all three but I am struck by the fact that McQuarrie's first question about the nature of hope focuses on hope as passion. What is passion? It is a curious emotion in that it embraces two contradictory notions: that of passivity or acceptance, such as in the Passion of Jesus Christ and that of strong emotion leading to action, such as a passion for photography.

Hope-Passion as Acceptance

The idea of hope-passion as acceptance, or allowing something merely to be, is open to misinterpretation and needs some further explanation, as it can be easily be interpreted as complacency or, even worse, as apathy. Passion, in the sense of passive acceptance, is the quality that marks the stance of the one in prayer before God, a quality which allows the unfolding of and movement towards union, a process which was started so long ago and, because of a variety of influences, remains unfinished. The attitude of allowing lets the unfinished business of infancy move towards completion. The meaning of hope-passion as passive acceptance underscores the paradox which is integral to the essence of passion. But a passivity expressed as letting things all hang out, without any formal structure, is not what I'm talking about here. Within and under the gaze of God lies the safety net, the "holding environment" (Winnicott) which keeps us safe.

In their writings on the process of separation/individuation by which the toddler individuates out of the mother-infant matrix, Margaret Mahler et al. point to the emotional (i.e. non-physical) holding which the mother provides which enables the infant to explore the environment, always under her watchful gaze. It is the mother's allowing her child to move outside the circle of her arms which facilitates the process by which the infant is able, gradually, and at times painfully, to move out of a symbiotic relationship with the mother towards psychological, if not physical, independence. The whole process of healthy emotional development depends on the crucial factor of non-interference on the part of the mother.

The passion/allowing, here as elsewhere, is better understood as a tolerance, where tolerance is understood as flexibility, play, or a latitude or a margin of freedom which allows not only room for manoeuvre but also room for growth. Acceptance refers to the creating of a space for play, or what Winnicott calls a potential space between the "me and the not-me." He notes,

> This potential space belongs to the change that has to be taken into consideration when the baby who is merged in with the mother feels the mother to be separated off.[22]

The process of psychological separation, a process fuelled by hope, is a process where the hopes of the mother are mirrored by the inarticulate hopes of the infant. This psychological separation of mother and infant is replicated in the spiritual domain by the separation of the soul from all that binds it to earthly concerns. The allowing, waiting, suffering experience becomes a sacred space between what is and what is to come. The prayer environment is also one where space is created in order to play, to make room for a play on words, to play with ideas, to play along. I frequently pose these

---

[22] D.W. Winnicott, *The Child, the Family and the Outside World* (London: Penguin, 1964) 146.

questions to those I accompany into the mystery of the Divine: "Do you allow God to have fun with you? Do you allow God to get down on his hands and knees, and play? Do you feel sufficiently free to play before the face of God, much in the same way that Wisdom does in the book of Proverbs: "I was by his side ... delighting him day after day; ever at play in his presence, at play everywhere in his world, delighting to be with the sons of men" (Prov. 8:30-31, JB). Or are you on your best behaviour and resort to all sorts of contrived language to speak with your Abba? Do you ask God to "vouchsafe" (whatever that means); "deign to look down graciously"; "attend mercifully to my petitions," and so on? If we spoke to our spouse, parents, or friends in this way, they would surely think that we had completely lost our minds.

The beautiful sense of passion as acceptance sets the scene for God to replicate in the adult those conditions established for the child by the good-enough mother who "does not hurry [her baby's] development and so enables him to catch hold of time, to get the feeling of an internal personal going on being."[23] Passion, in this sense, is, within the context of prayer,

---

[23] D.W. Winnicott, *Through Paediatrics to Psycho-Analysis,* 161.

the allowing, without rush, without pressure, without untoward intrusiveness.

Thus far, we have been considering the dimension of passion as acceptance and allowing. From the perspective of a prophetic orientation there is one final point to consider. The most important feature of passion as allowing acceptance is allowing room for God. The call of the prophet is the call to hope, that is, a trusting hope in what God can accomplish; it is a call that does not project its own view on the future or attempt to exercise control over it but rests in confidence on God's protection and help, thus opposing any human certainty and attempts at control. Healing comes with a quiet waiting on God (Is. 38:15; Ps. 36:5-7), and prayer becomes the practice of "the art of unknowing" (Kurtz).

Hope-Passion as Strong Emotion

This meaning of passion is one of strong emotion leading to action. In Peter Shaffer's play *Equus,* the case facing the psychiatrist, Martin Dysart, in his treatment of Alan Strang, a young man who had mutilated six horses by blinding them with a metal spike, was a similar quandary to one facing the poet

Rilke who abandoned therapy because of the fear that if his demons were exorcised, then his angels would also depart. For Dysart, removing the demons from Alan Strang would also rob him of his angels. In the final scene of the play Dysart agonizes over the task of separating out the destructive from the creative because both were unique features of Alan's personality. The psychiatrist flinches at the prospect of restoring the boy to normal, because he feels that by doing so, he will strip Alan of the capacity for passion and will be compelled to excise that very part which makes the boy an individual, possessed of properties and talents unique to himself, all in the service of the "Great God Normal." Dysart reflects, "The Normal is the good smile in the child's eyes all right. It is also the dead stare in a million adults. It both sustains and kills, like God. It is the Ordinary made beautiful: it is also the Average made lethal. The Normal is the indispensable, murderous God of Health, and I am his Priest" (19, 63).

In the final scene, when told by his friend Hesther that he can take away the boy's pain, he responds heatedly

> *All right! I'll take it away!* He'll be delivered from madness. *What then?* He'll feel himself acceptable! *What then?* ... My desire might be to make this boy an ardent

husband, a caring citizen, a worshipper of abstract and unifying God. My achievement, however, is more likely to make him a ghost! ...

I'll erase the welts cut into his mind by flying manes ... and give him Normal places for his ecstasy ... With any luck his private parts will come to feel as plastic to him as the products of the factory to which he will almost certainly be sent ... Hopefully, he'll feel nothing at his fork but Approved Flesh. *I doubt, however, with much passion!* ... Passion, you see, can be destroyed by a doctor. It cannot be created[24]

And this may well indeed lie at the heart of tragedy.

The semantics of suffering in this instance carry us close to the edge of the tragic dimension of the human condition. Passion, in this sense, is the core of the emotional life, strong emotion leading to action. Of course, in Alan Strang's case, his passion, his strong emotion, led to obscenely destructive activity, the act of blinding six horses which were supposedly witnesses to Alan's sexual shame. This is the sort of destructive and unreasoned passion that gets expressed in the antisocial tendency, the urge to involve society in the redressing of the evils of the past. This is, however, but one expression of a passionate impulse, the negative side which mirrors the more positive lust for life that lies at the root of the prophet's call.

---

[24] P. Shaffer, *Equus* (Athenium Press, 1973), 35, 105-106.

There is a raw energy in this idea of passion that seems more suitably expressed by a prophetic model than by the more idyllic image of the pastor, an image that perhaps doesn't fire the imagination in quite the same way and lacks the power, the urgency, and the immediacy of the prophetic call.

As we come to the end of this chapter, we enter into the general circular pattern of the book by returning to the place where we started, that is, by going back to the start of the chapter where we found the young woman in a wheelchair on the sanctuary of a Bradford church. Hers was the hope of patient waiting, a patient waiting which placed her squarely in line with the valiant women of the OT. In this woman's heart there surely must have been the passion of intense longing; perhaps more than a little envy of those around her who were sound of limb; maybe some bitterness that she should be physically challenged through no fault of her own; the pain and anger of being literally overlooked because she was not at the same eye-level as others and a constant longing for healing and inner peace.

Halina Birenbaum who was liberated from the Neustadt-Giewe concentration camp in 1945 wrote her memoirs of that experience to which she gave the title in its English translation *Hope Is the Last to Die,*[25] taken from a Japanese proverb. At the end of this chapter, we have wandered far in our exploration of the nature of hope. Perhaps, in certain life-threatening instances, hope is indeed the last to die but faith and hope and love always remain and the greatest of these is love. Our journey into the mystery of the Divine, always under the constant gaze of a loving God-Mother is one of unfolding; all we need to do is to show up and wait. When I worked for a child protection agency in Boston, Massachusetts I learned the inevitability of the legal system's delays leading to the motto, "Hurry up and wait." Whenever I was about to go before a judge at the Suffolk County Courthouse to appear on behalf of a client I realised the same may be applied to prayer: enter the mystery with alacrity and wait for it to unfold.

> But the faith and the love and the hope are all in the waiting.
> Wait without thought, for you are not ready for thought
> So the darkness shall be the light, and the stillness the dancing
> T. S. Eliot[26]

---

[25] H. Birenbaum, *L'espoir est le dernier à mourir.* Translated by Corinne Rouach (State Museum of Auschwitz-Birkenau, Oświęcim, 2008).
[26] T.S. Eliot, *Four Quartets*, 24, 25.

Chapter 3

Third Perspective:
Journey into Wholeness

How can I be substantial if I do not cast a shadow?
I must have a dark side also if I am to be whole.
C.G. Jung

Movement into wholeness is complex because it involves
a number of different kinds of transition, each involving a
separate movement, but each linked to and dependent upon
the others, much in the same way that individual petals of a
rose are distinct and separate but cannot exist independently,
either of the other petals or the stem from which each takes
nourishment. Bearing in mind that grace is built on nature,
and that all movement occurs under the loving gaze of God,
bearing in mind also that movement towards maturity and
movement towards closer union with God go hand in hand, we
must proceed with caution, because some parts of this chapter
deal with emotional and psychological development, and in
these parts, there are few explicit references to spiritual growth

and development; neither are there explicit references to God. In these parts of the chapter the life force which stimulates growth and development is always understood to be the all-embracing gaze of God.

The main thrust of this chapter is upon various types of movement, where each distinct movement draws us into greater freedom and wholeness. "Be all you can be." This aphorism, in Maslow's hierarchy of human needs, encapsulates the drive towards self-actualisation, which, according to Maslow, is the highest aspiration humans are capable of. Irenaeus, the second century bishop of Lyon, phrased it a little more elegantly with his maxim: *Gloria Dei homo vivens* (The Glory of God is human being fully alive).

Drawing upon the insights of a different academic discipline, that of pedagogy, we find that Malcolm S Knowles, in his book *The Modern Practice of Adult Education*, holds that maturity is the goal of education. He cites Harry Overstreet's *The Mature Mind* and notes, "A mature person is not one who has come to a certain level of achievement and stopped there. He is rather a *maturing* person, one whose *linkages with life* are constantly becoming stronger and richer because his attitudes are such as to encourage their growth."[1] Knowles goes on to observe, "Out of the psychological literature comes the notion that there are several dimensions of the maturing process, each with its own unique cycle of development." He proposes fifteen dimensions of the maturing process, of which three are germane to the present study: (i) movement from dependence towards autonomy; (ii) movement from self-rejection towards self-acceptance; (iii) movement from selfishness towards altruism. To these I would add two additional dimensions which Knowles does not include, namely, (iv) movement away from rigidity towards flexibility and (v) movement away from need to desire. We will explore these various movements, starting with the movement I consider to be foundational to all other movements, namely, the movement away from rigidity towards flexibility. The reason for this is because, in line with the theme of this book, flexibility is one of the characteristics of babyhood, and in our circularl journey into the mystery of the Divine, it is towards

---

[1] M.S. Knowles, *The Modern Practice of Adult Education*, (New York: Association Press, 1970) 25.

a recapturing of the primal relationship of infancy that we constantly move.

Before proceeding with an investigation into these conversion movements (and it is well to remember that conversion is a permanent process, or a cluster of different but interrelated processes), we need to address one of the implications of transition, namely, the fact that as we move away from one position to another, there is usually a feeling of loss: loss of security; loss of comfort; loss of assurance. As we move from one phase to another, we have to leave behind a prior way of being, much like a butterfly develops by moving from egg to larva to caterpillar to pupa and finally to adult butterfly. Or, as Paul describes it, "When I was a child, I spoke like a child, I thought like a child, I reasoned like a child; when I became a man, I gave up childish ways" (1 Cor. 13: 11).

As we move from phase to phase on the spiritual journey, often folding back on ourselves, often exposed to bleak winter moments when we long for the warmth and fecundity of summer, we have to leave behind those ways of being which provided comfort and security but which, if we cling to the attitudes, assumptions, and beliefs of a prior phase, impede movement into freedom. Movement from one state to another involves the sometimes painful experience of uncertainty, loss, and its corollary, emptiness, which, in turn, creates longing and awareness of our helplessness.

Movement from one state to another also involves a certain measure of resistance. Change is rarely comfortable, and the human organism responds with a certain degree of reluctance. As Kegan notes

> When the body tenses and defends against reorganisation, this causes greater pain than the reorganization itself. If we relax immediately after stubbing our toe the pain subsides. Our digging in and defending against the movements which make what-is what-was causes us pain. Any movement which sets us against the movement of life of which we are part, in which we are ultimately implicated, to which we are finally obligated, will cause us pain. In defence against the losses which have already occurred, in defence against the experience of grief and mourning we inflict on ourselves a pain which is greater than the loss itself.[2]

If defence against reorganisation causes such pain in the domain of the physical, how much more so does it cause pain in the spiritual sphere. The temptation remains, however, to cling to the familiar rather than move outside our comfort zone. The gaze of God is a constant prompting of love, which

---

[2] R. Kegan, *The Evolving Self* 266.

draws us out of a dependency upon the known and calls us to surrender and allow ourselves to become immersed in the cloud of unknowing, which stands between us and the Lord. Response to the call to abandonment, to radical loss, lies at the heart of all spiritual growth. This is because the experience of loss is the defining experience of our relationship with God: "Go from your country and your kindred and your father's house to the land that I will show you" (Gen. 12:1).

A sense of loss is vital to growth because the sense of emptiness engendered by loss becomes the soil in which the seed of God is planted; the barrenness of loss becomes the fount of creativity. As mentioned in the previous chapter, creation is the forming of the void, a womb of emptiness that becomes quickened to new life under the gaze of God. In the first account of creation in Genesis, the priestly author describes creation as an act of separation and, consequently, as the forming of a space between two opposing realities, order from chaos; light from darkness; waters beneath the firmament from waters above; dry land from water; the sun from the moon. The act of separation is a holy act, for the Hebrew word for holy translates into English as "separate" or "apart".

Looked at in this way, all development, be it physical or social, psychological or spiritual, involves separation from a prior state of being and, as an act of separation, is thereby holy. So when we resist the temptation to yearn metaphorically for the fleshpots of Egypt and commit ourselves to movement towards maturity, then we engage in something which is inherently holy and touched by the finger of God.

Once more, I would suggest that we think in terms of verbs (action words) rather than nouns (thing words) and understand the word 'separate' as an activity which is constant, vibrant, and unceasing, not an adjective describing a relationship of being different. "Behold, I am doing a new thing; now it springs forth, do you not perceive it? I will make a way in the wilderness and rivers in the desert" (Is. 43:19). And in Revelation, we read that the one on the throne said, "Behold, I make all things new" (Rev. 21:5). The Divine act of bringing to birth something new may be seen from the manner in which the Lord Jesus calls sinners, eats with them, finds pleasure in their company; this is why he tells stories about a lost sheep, a lost coin, a lost child. It is because, paradoxically, it is the very ones who are lost, the ones who are social pariahs shunned by the religious authorities, who are open to being recreated. The blind and the lame; the lepers and the pig-farmers; the prostitutes and the freedom fighters are made holy by their state of "sinfulness," by being separated from those who defend the prevailing religious attitudes of the day. The creative healing of the touch of God is accomplished only within the emptiness of the human heart, for it is only the empty who are filled with good things, while the rich are sent away empty.

As with physical growth, so it is with spiritual growth; it is the emptiness or space which allows for growth. The practice of fasting is not primarily a practice of self-denial; it has more to do with the awareness of emptiness and loss in which the possibility opens up of encounter with the Divine. Just as the experience of emptiness helps to focus attention, so too the experience of loss has a similar effect. In his biography of Dr Johnson, James Boswell notes, "Depend upon it, sir, when a man knows he is to be hanged in a fortnight, it concentrates his mind wonderfully."[3]

---

[3] J. Boswell, LLD, Vol. III.

What is so beautiful about this whole process is that emptiness begets longing, and our longing reaches out and touches the longing of God in a profoundly cosmic act of creation. This is what we find in Michelangelo's painting on the ceiling of the Sistine Chapel. The finger of God reaches out and almost touches the finger of Adam, and the space between them is the emptiness in which creation becomes possible.

It is the same longing in the heart of Hosea's God: "How can I give you up, O Ephraim! How can I hand you over, O Israel? ... My heart recoils within me, my compassion grows warm and tender" (Hos. 11:8). It is the same longing in the heart of Jesus, "O Jerusalem, Jerusalem, killing the prophets and stoning those who are sent to you. How often I would have gathered your children together as a hen gathers her brood under her wings and you would not" (Lk. 13: 24).

The Lord Jesus identifies Himself with the lost, the lonely, the outcast, as we read in the beautiful hymn Paul quotes in the second chapter of his letter to the Philippians, mentioned in the previous chapter: "who though he was in the form of God did not count equality with God a thing to be grasped, but emptied himself, taking the form of a servant, being born in the likeness of man" (Phil. 2:6-7).

One of the less endearing qualities in small children is their habit of constantly asking questions. Mothers can find themselves being asked hundreds of questions in the course of a single day: "Why is the sky blue? Why does God make some people black and others white? Why do I have two eyes but only one nose?" And it doesn't stop there; the questions continue into adulthood, as we wrestle with the need to make sense of our world. The human organism is a meaning-making machine; we need answers to the pressing conundrums of existence: Why do people starve when there is abundant food on our planet? Why do the innocent suffer? Why do children die? It is only where we encounter a gap in our knowledge that we seek meaning; otherwise, we just live in a taken-for-granted world, in a world unexamined in spite of its inconsistencies and inequalities. Jesus' embrace of the emptiness of death stands as a metaphor for the human need to make meaning from tragedy. Had Jesus, Son of God, not endured a shameful death, there would be no reason to question the goodness and compassion of God. It is not only that the contradictions of life provoke an urgent need to ascribe meaning by facing us with the void between what happens in our world and making sense of what happens, it is precisely into the emptiness of non-comprehension that meaning is inserted.

If I can put it in a less abstract way, the awareness of something missing makes us focus attention. "Where did I put the car keys?" "Have you seen my purse?"

Loss occasions an awareness of emptiness, of something missing, of an unoccupied space, but perhaps it is the very emptiness which allows us to construct meaning. Let me give a concrete example of how emptiness or space allows us to make meaning. What precisely gives meaning to the words on this page? The alphabet used, Roman instead of Greek or Hebrew? The language in which they are written? The way they are organised in the sentence? I venture to suggest that we are able to derive meaning from the words primarily because of space or emptiness. Take the sentence "The cat sat on the mat." Now, if I were to superimpose each individual letter one upon the other, you would be unable to understand what is written. What gives the sentence meaning is the space which occurs within each individual letter, the space between the letter, and the space between each word. You will get a sense of what I mean if you look at what is not there, instead of what is. Look at the white rather than the black; look at the space circumscribed by the shape and form of the letter rather than the printed letter itself. Then you will begin to appreciate the value of emptiness.

It gets even more complex when we consider the field of perception and interpretation, but that would take us outside the sphere of the present study. Suffice it to say that when we look at something, we automatically interpret what we see. And everyone interprets what they see differently. For example, standing in an airport waiting for a loved one to arrive, we see countless individuals who pass by who have no interest to us, but as soon as we see the person we are waiting for, we light up, whereas others who wait beside us look on with indifference. Our perceptions shape our interpretation of reality, and the many perceptions we have built up of God over time influence the way we interpret those perceptions, and our interpretations are rarely accurate. As it is with physical perception, so it is with the way we understand and interpret our relationship with God. We interpret our relationship with the Lord through a filter of a lifetime of experiences, and each one of us interprets that relationship differently. Not only that, we project on to God thoughts, feelings, ideas, and passing fancies, and we interpret God's response in the light of those projections. In short, unless we stick with the emptiness, unless we adopt the stance of silent waiting, we are deluding ourselves.

Let us now move on to a consideration of the various kinds of movement towards spiritual maturity, beginning with the movement from rigidity towards flexibility.

1. From rigidity towards flexibility

If you recall from the introduction that I regard spiritual development as a circular movement (or a series of movements) towards a condition we previously enjoyed at our mothers' breast, then you will appreciate that one of the properties of infancy is physical pliability and flexibility; infants, unlike most adults, find no difficulty in putting their toes in their mouths. Babies are incapable of holding up their heads, of sitting upright unaided; still less can they stand on their own. There is an essential floppiness to babies which makes them dependent on others to hold them. As we grow, we literally learn to stand on our own two feet, and we become independent, but as we develop our spiritual lives, we move beyond independence towards an inter-dependence with God Who always holds us in the light of His loving gaze.

Why is flexibility so important? For a variety of reasons. In the first place, human becoming is a process, and as a process, it demands a certain fluidity, a malleability, as it were. Just as a pot-bound plant may die unless it is given sufficient room to grow, so too if we cling rigidly to our own ideas and customs, we shall be less than we might be. Spiritual growth, like human development, like the universe itself, is a constant outward movement of expansion. When we were children, we were taken to the shoe shop for a new pair of shoes, usually in a larger size. If we tried to fit our feet into a size which felt comfortable a year ago, then we would be in the same position as Cinderella's ugly sister, who complained that her shoe was too tight. The same applies to the life of prayer; many people cling rigidly to a way of praying which was perfectly acceptable at a prior state of development. What happens is that they sometimes impede growth by thinking that their way of praying is the only way; others may feel that their way of praying no longer seems to be authentic. They wonder why the experience is no longer enriching and either continue out of a sense of duty orabandon the attempt as futile.

The foundational movement from rigidity towards increasing pliability is spiritual, emotional, and psychological as well as physical, a circular movement towards regaining that flexibility we previously enjoyed. So let's begin by considering certain aspects of this important journey away from rigidity towards flexibility and some of the difficulties we encounter on this particular journey.

The movement from rigidity to flexibility faces us with three fundamental problems. In the first place, early experiences become embedded in memory and largely shape later attitudes and behaviour patterns; therefore they are difficult to change. Particularly when we are tired or sad, we regress to earlier patterns of thought and behaviour, and because we have no means of testing our relationship with God (because He is silent and invisible) we can cling to immature ways of praying.

I remember vividly my mother's first attempts to teach me how to pray. Each Sunday, she would take me to church on the back of her bike. In the depths of winter, I would be absolutely frozen, and when we got to church, she would thaw out my tiny paws by putting them in her mouth. What sort of God demanded this sort of discomfort? Not one I was particularly keen on getting to know. Cold knees and frozen hands are no longer part of my prayer life. I think I have progressed slightly beyond that, but as the song says, "the song is ended but the melody lingers on" and there are occasions when, feeling lonely or misunderstood, I resort to ways of praying which are definitely less than adult. I can become petulant and aggrieved with the best of them.

The second problem is the way we read Scripture, particularly the Old Testament, which presents us with a God who is sometimes harsh, vengeful, and punitive. From such readings, we derive an image of God who is on the lookout to punish us if we have the temerity to step out of line. Consider the wife of Lot, who glanced over her shoulder to see the destruction of Sodom and Gomorrah and was turned into a pillar of salt (Gen. 19:26). The parable of the talents in

Matthew also portrays an image of God who is demanding and unforgiving. When the master settled accounts with the servants, he was wrathful towards the servant who buried the single talent in the ground: "You wicked and slothful servant. You know that I reap where I have not sowed and gather where I have not winnowed" And he cast the worthless servant into the outer darkness. There men will weep and gnash their teeth" (Mt. 25:26-30). There is an unfortunate tendency in the way we think in that we are sometimes inclined to look on the dark side and think negatively; we hedge our bets. If we were to interpret the parable benignly, then we would see it as an invitation to take risks with God and the riches He has endowed us with. In other words, the parable is an invitation to expand our vision of God and not interpret the Word too narrowly or too negatively.

The third problem concerns the confusion which arises if one identifies religion with spirituality or interprets spirituality as a function of religion. The word *religion* comes from the Latin *religare,* which means to bind again, to tie the mind and heart to an institution by requiring adherence to a set of rules and rituals. Also, all religions are types of organisation, and all organisations are structures. Salman Akhtar, in his *Comprehensive Dictionary of Psychoanalysis,* refers to David Rapaport's definition of an organisation as something which is "permanent or has a relatively slow rate of change." [4] Possessing as it does organisational properties, religions have a relatively slow rate of change and are inappropriate vehicles for something vibrant and dynamic, something constantly alive and changing, such as spiritual growth. If, as I believe, the primary purpose of the Son of God's becoming human was to proclaim the Good News, and at the heart of the Good News is the call to freedom, then anything which restricts or inhibits movement into freedom must be viewed with a certain amount of suspicion.

The need to keep religion and spiritual development separate was impressed upon me in the mid-eighties, when I began training in spiritual direction at the Center for Religious Development in Cambridge, Massachusetts. I was told that when working with clients, I must not wear a clerical collar or anything identifying me as a priest. The reason for this was

---

[4] S. Akhtar, *Comprehensive Dictionary of Psychoanalysis,* (London: Karnic Books, 2009) 272.

because the client might have assumptions about priests, which might hinder spiritual development. Secondly, priests, within a religious context, are usually regarded as authority figures which, if accepted as such by the client, would create an unequal relationship when the relationship between client and director is one of partnership in which both are on an equal footing as they move into the mystery of the Divine.

It is difficult to give an adequate definition of religion. Wulff points out that a satisfactory definition of religion has "eluded scholars to this day."[5] That being said, there are elements within the structure of all religions which militate against a movement into personal freedom. In a very brief overview of these elements, we may discern the following:

a) Religions introduce prescriptions and proscriptions. Religion defines a relationship between human beings and God which, through prescribing certain actions, such as attendance at church, mosque, synagogue, or temple and proscribing others, such as lying and cheating, impose a measure of control. Religions frequently present a view of

---

[5] D.M. Wulff, *Psychology of Religion: Classical and Contemporary,* 2nd Edition, (New York: John Wiley and Sons,1997) 3.

the deity as one who demands propitiation, submission, atonement, fealty, and obedience in order that human beings may escape unpleasant consequences: "Do this and you shall live" (Gen. 42:18; Lev. 18: 5; Lk. 10: 28). In order to placate the divinity, one must do certain things and avoid doing other things. The realm of the spiritual, by contrast, is one which leads into freedom, not servitude.

b) Religions foster an "us and them" attitude which has led to religious persecutions down through the ages. Early Christians were fed to the lions because of their beliefs; the Crusades were wars motivated by religion; Catholics were persecuted by Protestants in England during the Reformation; and Catholics persecuted Protestants in France. Still the conflict born of religious practices and beliefs continues today. Meriam Ibrahim, a Sudanese woman, was condemned to death by the authorities for apostasy although she was brought up as a Christian; she was sentenced to a hundred strokes of the lash for adultery because she married a Christian, and it was only the expression of universal outrage which prompted the Sudanese authorities to commute the sentence

c) Religions can foster entrenched attitudes which, in turn, can lead to prejudice and intolerance. James Alcock writes,

> Most religions encourage the faithful to love one another and all humanity, and yet many also promote the idea that only their adherents possess God's truth, thus promoting a sense of self-righteousness and a belief that those not of the faith are in error and in need of conversion. Intolerance of nonbelief and deviance is thereby fostered: if scripture proscribes homosexuality, then homosexuals should be treated as sinners.... Indeed, Alport found that churchgoers in the 1950s harbored *more* ethnic prejudice than non-churchgoers.[6]

We have seen some of the negative properties of organised religion. But that is only half the picture. The other half of the picture shows religion as a force for good and stability, providing what Winnicott terms a holding environment. Religion has the capacity to provide comfort, solace, and security.

A more congenial property of religion is that it holds us securely and keeps us safe in our relationship with God. When we experience ourselves as being held securely in His love, paradoxically, we are free to wander in spirit, thus recapturing what occurred physically and emotionally in our

---

[6] J.E. Alcock, "Religion and Rationality," In *Religion and Mental Health,* Ed. John F. Schumaker (Oxford University Press, 1992) 127.

early stages of human development. Margaret Mahler et al., in *The Psychological Birth of the Human Infant,* note that in the separation-individuation process we all go through in the first eighteen months of life, there are different sub-phases of development. The central feature of the second sub-phase is "the elevated investment in the exercise of the autonomous functions, especially motility, to the near exclusion of apparent interest in the mother at times."[7] The same applies to our relationship with God. And here again lies the rub.

We are aware that much of the prayer of the church with its ritual and liturgy is formal and inflexible. This has certain advantages, in that we all pray in unison and sing from the same page of the hymn book, using the same forms of archaic and outmoded language, accompanied by the same formal gestures. It is little wonder that many youngsters, familiar with the practically limitless possibilities of expression offered by the internet, find the verbal and bodily restrictions imposed by church services to be lifeless, alien, and, as many complain, boring.

---

[7]   M. Mahler, F. Pine, and A. Bergman, *The Psychological Birth of the Human Infant,* (New York: Basic Books, 1975) 69.

But that is the liturgical world of church services. Private prayer is a different kettle of fish. The problem arises when we apply the same criteria appropriate to church services to personal prayer. Commitment to spiritual growth takes us along pathways different from those offered by organised religion. Spiritual development promotes freedom and flexibility, recapturing as it does the malleability and resilience of infancy. Who knows? One day, we may even achieve sufficient flexibility to be able to put our spiritual big toe into our spiritual mouth and roll around the floor in delight.

"Unless you turn and become like children, you will never enter the kingdom of heaven" (Mt. 18: 3). The command is not only to become as little children but to "turn," that is, be converted, which, as we know, is a permanent process leading to the recaptured mind of a child. This does not imply that we adopt an uncritical and sentimental appraisal of childhood with all its wide-eyed wonder and innocence. Children, as we well know, can be little devils full of malice and ingratitude. We have to be selective in appropriating those features of childhood which enhance our prospects of gaining entry into the Kingdom, and one of those features which best serve our purpose is the spontaneity of the child. Sometimes, outbursts of spontaneity can have a negative side and can be embarrassing, such as when a child makes a loud comment like "Why is Aunt Mary wearing such a funny hat?" But at least the comment is honest and direct, two of the worthy characteristics of a healthy prayer life. The measure of spontaneity indicates the level of freedom we bring to prayer.

2. From self-rejection towards self-acceptance

During my novitiate, I had a rather zealous vice-master who, on more than one occasion, made me kneel before him due to some infringement of novitiate rules. He would then wag his finger at me and tell me that I was full of pride and that he was going to corkscrew it out of me. Sad to say, he didn't quite succeed. Unfortunately, so much Christian spiritual writing reinforces a negative self-understanding, one which has little to do with our standing as beloved children of God. Like a boy who is told to write a thank-you note to an aunt who had given him a pair of socks for his birthday, when what he really wanted was a model aeroplane, we are constantly being reminded that we should always be grateful for something for which we are not truly thankful. At the beginning of each Eucharistic celebration, the eternal act of gratitude to the Father, we are called upon to acknowledge our failings. How on earth can we come freely and with light hearts before the throne of grace if we are constantly apologising for some real or imagined transgressions?

In the introduction I alluded to the story of the Fall in Genesis where God calls Adam and Eve out of hiding and covers their shame with His gentle love. The Genesis story is a reminder that the spiritual journey upon which we embark is a response to the voice of God, who calls us out of hiding. We are constantly being called to emerge from the dark undergrowth of our imagined failures to live up to unreal expectations we place upon ourselves. "I shouldn't be so lazy; so selfish; so self-opinionated; so materialistic; so judgmental; so lustful; so self-indulgent", and so on. It's enough to make God weep. According to Jung, the process of being called out of hiding is called individuation. This process is one whereby we become human to the extent to which consciousness differentiates out of an unconscious matrix and, over time, moves towards integration and wholeness.

As Jung writes

> In actual life ... acceptance of oneself is the essence
> of the moral problem and the acid test of one's whole
> outlook on life. That I feed the beggar, that I forgive an
> insult, that I love my enemy in the name of Christ-all
> these are undoubtedly great virtues. But what if I should
> discover that the least among them all are within me, and
> that I myself stand in need of my own kindness, that I
> myself am the enemy who must be loved, what then?[8]

There lurk deep within us dark unconscious forces, which Jung calls the shadow. They describe movements of anger and resentment which surface into consciousness and leave us uncomfortable, distressed, and ashamed. It is not primarily the nature of these outbursts that affect us; it is rather the intensity and inappropriate-ness of the feelings which are so unsettling. If these feelings remain rejected and are regarded as unacceptable, they become broken-off parts of the self and, like jagged splinters, wound our souls. If, on the other hand, we can accept them as part of who we are, then their power is thereby diminished, and as we integrate these feelings into who we are, they are robbed of their intensity. "Make friends quickly with your accuser while you are going with him to

---

[8] C.G, Jung, *Psychology and Religion: West and East* (Princeton University Press and Routledge & Kegan Paul) 519, 520.

court, lest your accuser hand you over to the judge." (Mt. 5:25). And, as Jung maintains, the shadow gives substance to our being: "How can I be substantial if I do not cast a shadow? I must have a dark side also if I am to be whole."

3. From dependence to autonomy

At the beginning of the chapter, I used the metaphor of a rose to illustrate the interdependence upon one another of the various forms of psychological development; the individual petals of a rose are distinct and separate but cannot exist independently of the other petals or the stem from which each takes nourishment, so too, forms of emotional and spiritual development are interdependent, much in the same way as breathing and blood circulation are linked in the living organism. All forms of the maturation process are interrelated and overlap.

In this section, we shall turn our attention towards the movement from dependence towards autonomy. The path to autonomy is one of separation, of cutting the ties which bind. Our progress towards spiritual as well as physical, emotional, and psychological maturity depends on our ability to relinquish the metaphorical ties to our mothers' apron strings and move into a world of doubt. Physical, emotional, and spiritual growth, are determined by the extent to which we have moved from a position of dependence towards autonomy, a position from which we can acknowledge and act upon our interdependence not only with other people but also with the whole of created reality. We begin life totally dependent upon the care of others to provide for our basic physical and emotional needs. This absolute dependence brings with it a sense of insecurity and inchoate anxiety, which sometimes is difficult to assuage.

One of my earliest memories is of kneeling in a cot with flaking blue paint on its rails. It was an early summer morning, and I remember feeling so very anxious. Seeking reassurance, I repeatedly asked my mother, who was lying in her bed next to my cot, if she loved me. Like any child, I seemed to be in constant need of reassurance, and no amount of affirmation on my mother's part would allay the doubt. Like any small child, I lived in a world of insecurity. I couldn't dress myself; I couldn't feed myself; literally couldn't stand on my own two feet. Aware at some level that I was dependent on others brought with it a sense of vulnerability and a need for assurance. To be firmly held, both physically and emotionally, is vital to the psychological as well as the physical well-being of the baby.

Deprived of that security which comes from adequate holding, the baby experiences profound anxiety which, occurring as it does at the first stage of emotional development, is necessarily primitive, threatening, and therefore terrifying. As infants, we needed repeated experiences of being cared for by someone who is dependable in order to build a sense of trust in an environment as essentially friendly. As we saw in the first chapter, trust is the primary and foundational achievement of human and spiritual development. Without basic trust, infants are deprived of the essential tools to resolve the next stage of Erikson's psychosocial development, the crisis of resolving the tension between autonomy and shame and doubt.

Erikson, in his second stage, points to the developmental crisis which begins around eight months, which consists in the struggle between holding on and letting go. It is a battle between elimination and retention, which finds its basic expression in the activity of the sphincter, the muscle which controls the alternating movement between rigidity and relaxation, between elimination and retention. It is a time of the beginnings of self-control; it is a time of nascent self-awareness, when the child starts to differentiate between the "me" and the "not-me." It is a time for hoarding things as a demonstration of possession and control, and a time for throwing things out of the car window (which for parents can be extremely irritating).

When children fail to build a sense of control, a sense of autonomy over theiractions, a sense of shame or guilt sets in. Effective parenting, according to Erikson, calls for parents to treat their child with firmness and tolerance. "Be firm and tolerant with the child at this stage, and he will be firm and tolerant with himself. He will feel pride in being an autonomous person, he with grant autonomy to others, and now and again, he will even let himself get away with something."[9]

---

[9]   E.E. Erikson, In Lewis and Volkmar, *Cliical Aspects of Child and Adolescent Development*, (Lea and Febiger, 1990) 91.

The road to autonomy is paved with the mistakes we make along the way. The reason for this is because we do not have a blueprint, a map which determines the route of the journey towards what it means to be fully human, fully alive, so we are bound to get things wrong from time to time. Of course, there are guidelines to help us, social conventions, legal, ethical and religious prescriptions and proscriptions which serve as boundaries to keep us safe. The journey towards autonomy, as Paul so often writes, is one no longer subject to law so the boundaries the law provides are permeable and flexible. As Erikson notes, the autonomous person "now and again ... will even let himself get away with something."

The problem emerges, however, at those times when we (or more significantly, authority figures) ascribe a moral value to the mistakes we make and call them sinful. Unfortunately, in the world of religion, ritual and dogma do not lend themselves to autonomy or self-determination. And it is both ritual and dogma which largely shape religious, if not spiritual, thinking and behaviour, dominated as it is by the belief that it is only by the imposition of control that souls will be saved: "Do this and you shall live." And by doing so, we become subservient and yield our autonomy.

Movement towards autonomy is such that a response to the demands of external authority which emanates from a personal decision born of freedom is vastly different from unquestioning acquiescence. The autonomous person responds positively to rules and regulations and the demands of legitimate authority from a position of internal strength, which is not only a human response but, more importantly, one which is illuminated by the light of the Spirit; it is a response which comes from faithfulness to the covenant with the Lord and is made expressly under the gaze of God.

There is, however, another facet to the temptation to surrender autonomy, and that is the temptation to cling to the certainty it provides, a certainty which relieves us of the demands of thinking for ourselves and making our own decisions. This certainty, this assurance provided by total reliance upon external authority, may lead to a certain arrogance of being right all the time. This was the belief of the Scribes and Pharisees. What prevented many of them from responding to Jesus' invitation to move into life and freedom was their being so sure of themselves, so sure of their traditions, so sure of their rectitude. It's not that they were bad people; it was just that they were blind to the possibilities of life and freedom. "Woe to you, blind guides, who say, 'If any one swears by the temple, it is nothing; but if any one swears by the gold of the temple, he is bound by his oath.' You blind fools" (Mt. 23:16). The apostles themselves were not immune to their own prejudices. For instance, when Philip went in search of Nathaniel, to tell him they had found the one Moses and the prophets wrote of, Jesus of Nazareth, Nathaniel's response comes out of his own narrow world of certainty: "Can anything good come out of Nazareth?" (Jn. 1:46).

Because we inhabit a universe which is constantly expanding, because we are caught up in an evolutionary process which is constantly in a state of flux, there are only two things, as the old saying goes, we can be certain of: death and taxes. If we are physically caught up in perpetual motion, and if the human species is evolving into a higher form of being, then any thought or action which locks us into an inflexible way of looking at ourselves and our world will necessarily delay our own becoming and delay the coming of Christ.

The call to freedom is a call to let go of our own certitude because, basically, our certitude may well stem from laziness of thought and lack of tolerance (tolerance in the sense of flexibility and play). In the beautiful sequence for Pentecost, we pray to the Spirit, *"Flecte quod est rigidum,"* asking the Spirit to bend what is rigid, a prayer for increased flexibility in the way we accept ourselves, the way we show tolerance for others, and how we bring a light touch to the way we interact with our world. This call to freedom is how Gerald May interprets the dark night of the soul of John of the Cross:

> Regardless of when and how it happens, the dark night of the soul is the transition from bondage to freedom in prayer and in every other aspect of life. In prayer, the movement is from the personal control and effort that characterises meditation to the willingness and simple being that characterises contemplation. As one becomes less willful and controlling in prayer, so one also grows in willingness and trust in the rest of life.[10]

A willingness to embrace the confusion born of a lack of certitude leads us into the realm of ambiguity and ambivalence. It invites us to move more deeply into The Cloud of Unknowing, which exposes us to the basic ambivalence we hold in our hearts with regard to our relationship with God.

---

[10] G. May, *The Dark Night of the Soul,* (Harper Collins e-books) 131.

In terms of emotional development, ambivalence concerns the ability to acknowledge that we can love and hate the same person at the same time. One major indication of movement towards maturity in the spiritual life is the ability to acknowledge, if not our hatred of God, then at least our anger towards Him. It is frustrating at times to enter into the presence of someone who is all-powerful, is all-knowing, and, what hurts most, is always right. To acknowledge our negative feelings towards God is a sign of maturity and usually occurs at those times when we are disappointed that He doesn't seem to be listening to our prayer; does not grant our very reasonable requests; is seemingly judgmental or critical of our uncharitable or lustful thoughts. Because God is a totally blank screen, we project our own negative thoughts and feelings onto him. We then may experience feelings of guilt, which compound the difficulty, saying to ourselves, "I shouldn't be feeling like this. I should be grateful for all that God has given me." Then feelings of resentment may emerge, feelings that we are trying our best but getting absolutely nowhere.

Our ambivalence towards God intensifies at those times when we are tired or stressed or lonely or off-balance. At those times, we regress to childish ways and, metaphorically, stamp our foot like an angry child who shouts at the mother, "I hate you! I hate you!" But we can't do that with God, or can we? When we shouted, "I hate you," at our mother, she didn't retaliate; nor was she destroyed by our anger and frustration. And so it is with God. When we go to prayer, we cannot pretend; when we go to prayer, it is always in response to the invitation to come as we are, warts and all. Trying to hide our hostility or disappointment or dissatisfaction with God is futile, as we well know. The ability to express our negative thoughts and feelings towards God is something of a subtle compliment. We are saying that we trust God sufficiently to put up with our tantrums and not take offence. The ability, then, to acknowledge our displeasure with God is an act of trust.

Such was the case with Teresa of Avila, who in 1578 fell down a flight of stairs in St Joseph's convent in Avila and broke her left arm. She is alleged to have cocked her eye to heaven and said, with a wry smile, "Lord, it's no wonder you have so few friends when you treat them the way you do." Now that is the freedom of familiarity which allows the mystic to say whatever comes into her head, knowing she would never cause offence.

Before leaving this section, there is another point to consider. Self-acceptance is particularly important when we come before God in prayer. It is not very helpful if we beat ourselves up because we are dry, inattentive, restless, or distracted. These feelings are all part of what it means to be human. One of the complaints I frequently hear is one of distractions at prayer. "I try to stay focused. I light a candle to help me, but my mind wanders hither and thither. I cannot seem to keep my mind on what I am doing." It feels somewhat shaming and guilt-provoking to become preoccupied with mundane affairs when at prayer. If we can view these distractions in the light of normal human development, we may see distractions, preoccupations, concerns, and worries which afflict us in time of prayer as but a re-emergence of a particular phase of psychological development, the phase which occurs between ten and twelve months, and sixteen and eighteen months. It is a time characterised by Phyllis Greenacre as the beginning of "a love affair with the world."[11] We bear within us vestiges of each phase of psychological

---

[11] P. Greenacre, "The Childhood of the Artist: Libidinal Phase Development and Giftedness," In *The Psychoanalytic Study of the Child,* Vol. 12 (New York: International Universities Press, 1957) 27ff.

development, and this particular phase is characterised by the ability to walk, to explore, to assert one's independence and individuality.

At times, at some unconscious level, we may well experience the presence of God as somewhat intrusive, and it is natural that we should lay claim to our own autonomy. Besides, the ability to walk contains the ability to wander, to meander, to ramble and flit about. This physical ability extends into the realm of the mind which, too, claims for itself the corresponding capacity for wandering. Distractions are simply clouds which drift across the face of the sun. When a shadow crosses our path, we don't switch on every light in the house; neither do we take a broom and attempt to sweep it away. God is always drawing us to Himself, and if we have that generosity of spirit to be present or, as St Teresa would have it, to waste time graciously with God, we wouldn't be unduly worried by idle thoughts which come into our minds. Let's face it, in prayer, there are no such things as distractions because all that is, all that exists, are channels through which we gain access to the living God. As we well know, but tend to forget from time to time, God does not confine his activity to inside the walls of the temple, church, synagogue, or mosque. God is everywhere. Distractions are nothing but opportunities to engage more richly with the Divine. "I mustn't forget to buy some milk because we are nearly out. I wonder what's on television tonight. Did I remember to record that programme? Time seems to be dragging; has my watch stopped?" All we need to do is to invite God in: "Lord, thank you that there is so much milk available to me when my sisters and brothers in other parts of your world do not have easy access. Remember the farmers. You used them as examples in so many of your stories. They must have a tough job in all winds and weathers. Be with them and protect them and give them a fair price for their milk."

Allowing God to come with us where our thoughts take us is a sign of growth and flexibility. It is also, more importantly, a sign that we are comfortable in our own skin before God and not afraid to be vulnerable. We can only say to God, "Take me as I am," if first we have come to the point of taking ourselves as we are. If we do violence to ourselves, dragging our wandering minds back, beating ourselves up for a lack of attention, then prayer ceases to be much fun and becomes onerous. Chill out. Don't take yourself too seriously.

4. From need to desire

This movement is the most difficult, the most problematic, the most arduous of all the movements into wholeness and the least understood. Broadly speaking, it is the movement away from preoccupation with the self towards total absorption in the other. Whereas need describes a lack of something necessary, requisite, or desirable for the well-being of an organism, desire describes an all-consuming impulse towards an object outside the self. Need describes the absorption - both physical and emotional - of what is not me into me, whereby I gain a sense of self. Need, when not in the service of self-preservation, soon degenerates into greed; it can well drain other people and drain the limited resources of the planet. One of the more damning comments one person can make about another is, "I try to avoid her because she is so needy."

Desire, on the other hand, is the affirmation of the other as subject, and whereas the root of need is greed, the root of desire is love, resting as it does upon the acknowledgement of the other as a subject worthy of reverence and respect. Desire is literally an ecstatic thrust in that it moves us outside the self and focuses exclusively on the other. In the context of spiritual growth, desire is a forgetfulness of self, as it finds its centre in the beloved. As we read in *The Cloud of Unknowing*:

> See to it that there is nothing at work in your mind or will but only God. Try to suppress all knowledge and feeling of anything less than God, and trample it down deep under the cloud of forgetting. You must understand that in this business you are to forget not only all other things than yourself (and their doings and your own!) but to forget also yourself, and even the things you have done for the sake of God.[12]

We might gain a clearer understanding of the movement from need to desire if we look at the structure of the Lord's Prayer. The beginning of the prayer in Matthew's Gospel (Mt. 6:9), "Our Father who art in heaven," immediately transports us from time into eternity and from the here-and-now of human concerns into the mystery of the Divine. Immediately forgetful of self, the words orientate us towards the future, wherein lies the fulfilment of human becoming. As Paul reminds us in his letter to the Philippians, "For us, our

---

[12] *The Cloud of Unknowing*, (Harmondsworth, Middlesex, Penguin Books, 1981), Chapter 43, 110.

homeland is in heaven, and from heaven comes the saviour we are waiting for, the Lord Jesus Christ" (Phil. 3:20, J.B.). Following the initial statement in the Lord's Prayer are seven petitions, the first three of which are petitions of desire, of ache, of longing which God alone can ease. The longing of the human heart expands the spirit and allows God greater space, if you will, in which to accomplish the in-breaking of the kingdom in our hearts. Prayer has been described as a loving personal encounter with God, and it is through being present to Him that we render ourselves capable of receiving. Each time we present ourselves before God, we become a little more sensitised to His loving presence; each time we present ourselves before the Lord, the void at the very core of our being becomes larger, wider, deeper, into which, if I may put it concretely, a greater portion of the infinite love of God may find a home.

The first three petitions of the Lord's Prayer stem from our relationship with God as *Abba,* child with father and lover with beloved; they are incredibly intimate. They are expressions of desire: thirst for reverence for God by all created reality; yearning for the kingship of God to be universally acknowledged; longing for infinite love to flood the earth with its healing power. Even the fourth petition, "Give us this day our daily bread," may be interpreted differently. Instead of looking at this petition as voicing physical need, we may understand it differently if we link it to verse 31 where we read, "Do not be anxious, saying, 'What shall we eat?' or 'What shall we drink?' … your heavenly Father knows that you need them all. But seek first his kingdom and his righteousness, and all these things shall be yours as well" (Mt. 6:31-33).

With eyes set on the coming kingdom, we submerge our needs beneath the waves of Divine compassion and embrace the process of conversion away from need to the desire for the fulfilment of the will of God. From the perspective of desire, the petition for daily bread may point not to "the simple provision of daily basic needs but to the ultimate realization of the reign in which basic daily needs cease to exist."[13] First and foremost, we are called to seek the kingdom of God and leave the rest in the hands of infinite love. If our focus in

---

[13] J.L. McKenzie, SJ, "The Gospel According to Matthew," In *The Jerome Biblical Commentary,* Edited by Raymond F Brown et al., (London, Geoffrey Chapman,1969) 73.

prayer remains centred upon self and our own needs, then we block off the channel through which the Spirit of God moves. When prayer is motivated by desire, a highway opens into the mystery of the Divine; when motivated by need, the paths become blocked and can only grow clear when we surrender ourselves to the process of conversion.

At the beginning of this section, I pointed out that this particular form of conversion is immensely difficult. One of the difficulties lies in the fact that our needs are pressing and seemingly unrelated to our life of prayer. And need may be simply the wish to have our curiosity satisfied; nothing wrong with that, surely? But as they say, curiosity killed the cat. At the end of John's Gospel, Jesus asks Peter a threefold question, "Do you love me?" Jesus follows with a threefold affirmation and commission to feed the sheep and the lambs. And after this he said to him 'Follow me" and then Peter turns round and sees the beloved disciple and asks "What about this man?" To which Jesus responds, "If it is my will that he remain until I come, what is that to you? Follow me!" (Jn. 21:22).

Here, Peter demonstrates a classic example of the difference between need and desire. By attempting to satisfy his curiosity, he turned. And by turning, he ceased to follow the Lord because he broke the gaze of God by looking in the opposite direction. We cannot walk forward if our glance is directed over our shoulder. However, there must be hope for the rest of us if Peter can take his eye off the ball and still attain some form of sanctity.

One of the dominant themes of this book is the importance of keeping our eyes fixed on God, never breaking the gaze, allowing ourselves to be drawn into the mystery of the Divine, the mystery of all-embracing love. As Teresa put it so succinctly with lines written in her breviary,

> Let nothing disturb thee, Nothing affright thee. All things are passing; God never changeth; Patient endurance Attaineth to all things; Who God possesseth In nothing is wanting. Alone God sufficeth.[14]

5. From selfishness to altruism

Altruism is possibly the best indicator of sound mental health. Where altruism is an expression of love, it is certainly the best indicator of spiritual health. Having said that, we must be very careful in how we approach this particular movement

---

[14] From *Hispanic Anthology: Poems Translated from the Spanish by English and North American Poets*. Collected and arranged by Thomas Walsh (New York: G. P. Putnam's Sons, 1920).

because altruism is often confused with selflessness, where individual needs are submerged in the service of the other and where this service is interpreted as the will of God. Take the example of a young woman who denies herself the prospect of a loving relationship in marriage in order to take care of an infirm parent. She yields her whole future as hostage and by doing so fails to nurture her spirit by allowing it to expand and grow and, as a result, becomes less than she might otherwise have been.

At the other end of the spectrum, there is an unfortunate tendency in human nature to attempt to incorporate what is not me into the me, a topic we covered earlier with reflections on need. In the life of prayer, this is demonstrated by a greater focus on petition than upon intercession. We are all good at the "gimme" prayer; this way of interpreting our world from a perspective of self impedes growth into the mystery of the Divine. One of the problems we face, at least in the West, is that not only do we begin life as self-centred little monsters but that movement away from focus upon the "me" to the "not-me" is made more difficult by the fact that Western culture encourages independence and cultivates the worth of the individual, largely to the detriment of group interests. Competition is favoured over collaboration from a very early age, whether in the field of academia or that of sport. There appears to be little room for deference, and, without deference, there is no possibility for the growth of reverence; there is no room for a deep respect for the other, a respect which mirrors the reverence in which God holds the whole of creation. To the extent we immerse ourselves in attitudes of reverence and humility, we are immersed in the heart of God.

If we are able to understand ourselves to be part of a universe which is constantly expanding, then our physical, mental, and spiritual growth depends on our willingness to be caught up in the eternal movement of expansion. This is a willingness based upon humility in its literal sense of earthiness, acknowledging that we are of the earth, that we are part of a tremendously diverse and delicate ecology, that we are not the centre of the universe. It is based on a sense of reverence towards all things of the earth, both animate and inanimate; it is assent to the fact that we are caretakers of our environment and a commitment to husbandry with regard to the planet's limited resources.

As we become more altruistic, our spirits expand and our perspectives enlarge, and we gaze upon all that is with a profound empathy. Mark Twain wryly illustrates the movement away from self-absorption towards a more inclusive perspective on life with his comment about his father. "When I was a boy of fourteen, my father was so ignorant I could hardly stand to have the old man around. But when I got to be twenty-one, I was astonished at how much the old man had learned in seven years."

Altruism differs from empathy because there is a certain sacrificial quality to altruism, whereas with empathy, we feel with the other but do not necessarily act on those feelings. Altruism involves outreach of a practical nature, such as sacrificing one's time for the benefit of the other or giving money to charitable causes. It carries with it an understanding that the gifting of self and possessions in the service of others is done with no wish for reward. The gifting of self is a *kenosis*, a self-emptying, which, as with other forms of conversion and growth, widen the spirit and enlarge our capacity to receive the in-breaking of God. Altruism becomes not only concrete in the gifting of self but, together with reverence and humility, becomes an underlying attitude which pours forth into our lives like a waterfall of grace. Contact with the Divine through personal prayer is essential; otherwise, the stream is reduced to a trickle or dries up altogether. But if we remain constant and faithful to time of silent prayer, we become rich heirs to the promise "whoever drinks of the water that I shall give will never thirst; the water that I shall give will become a spring of water welling up to eternal life" (Jn. 4:14).

Altruism flows from an understanding of self based on an awareness that we are one with the whole of created reality, that everything we own is but loaned to us for the duration of our lives, however short or long; that we stem from an origin which we share with all that is both animate and inanimate. Altruism is the price we pay back for the privilege of life; it is the gratitude we express for our being gifted with the ability to see, to hear, to speak, and to smell; it is the thankfulness, our very personal Eucharist, which we articulate on a daily basis for our food and drink, for clothing and shelter. Altruism is our acknowledgement that, irrespective of colour or creed, we are all children of the living God, and as His children we share our toys with our sisters and brothers with a profound generosity of heart.

In the spirit of the cyclical movements which lie at the heart of this book, we come again to the place where we started at the beginning of the chapter, with the aphorism of Irenaeus, *Gloria Dei homo vivens.* God's glory is vibrant and active to the degree to which we become fully alive. This we do by allowing Him to lead us along paths towards human maturity.

We began with a consideration of the movement from dependence towards autonomy, where we took the path towards increasing responsibility for our own thoughts and actions. Then we followed the path from self-rejection towards self-acceptance. This path led us to a more embracing acceptance of self in contrast to a negative and rejecting appraisal of ourselves. The next path led us from selfishness towards altruism, where we acknowledged our oneness with all created reality and responded, under the gaze of God, with reverence and gratitude.

Along the way, we took a couple of side trips, because the journey into union with God is not linear but circular and permits the exploration of other paths and other ways. That being said, we then investigated the movement away from rigidity towards flexibility, with the intention of loosening us up a bit in our understanding of our relationship with God. Finally, we took the path which leads away from need to desire. There we came full circle for desire, the focus on the good of the other, brought us face to face with the necessity of acknowledging and responding to the good of the other, which is the essence of altruism.

The next chapter will explore the experience of wilderness, our own personal encounter with the deserts in our lives. The misfortunes, the shadows, the failures, the grief which so often mark our passage through life also are places where we encounter the Divine. In the ninth chapter of John's Gospel, Jesus and His disciples meet a man blind from birth, and the disciples ask Jesus was it the man himself or his parents who sinned that he should be afflicted in that way. To which Jesus replied, "It was not that this man sinned, or his parents, but that the works of God may be made manifest in him" (Jn. 9:3).

Perhaps the next chapter will help open our eyes a little to a vision of our desert experiences of affliction as places where we encounter the mystery of the Divine and that the plan of God may be worked more visibly and more productively in our lives.

Chapter 4

The Fourth Perspective
Journey into Wilderness

No man can live this life [in the desert] and emerge unchanged.
He will carry, however faint, the imprint of the desert,
the brand which marks the nomad.
-Wilfred Thesiger, *Arabian Sands*

In the first three chapters, I have attempted to lay a foundation intended to provide a sufficiently secure base from which to face the challenges of the present chapter in all their rigour and harshness. The first three chapters, in other words, provide the sustenance necessary for the journey into wilderness. When Elijah entered the wilderness to escape the wrath of Jezebel, he wished to die, but then "behold an angel touched him, and said to him, 'Arise and eat else the journey will be too great for you.' And he arose and ate and drank, and went in the strength of that food forty days and forty nights to Horeb the mount of God" (1K. 19:7-8). Much of the preceding chapters have, I hope, not lulled you into a false sense of security about the journey into the mystery of the Divine but have provided nourishment, food for the metaphorical journey to Horeb, the mountain of God. Inescapably, the journey has to pass through the desert, so we need to have the necessary equipment before we set off. It is only when we have built a trusting and hope-filled relationship with God that we can face with confidence the aridity of wilderness experiences in whatever form they take in our daily lives.

It is one thing to give notional assent to the idea that the passage to union with God takes us through the desert; it is a different kettle of fish altogether to experience the desert wastes in the depths of our being. Perhaps, without intending to, we may make glib assumptions in which we can readily acknowledge in principle the need to enter wilderness in order to make progress on our spiritual journey, but it is altogether another matter when the real darkness falls into our lives, when we are exposed to the barrenness of the desert wastes in the concrete experiences of loneliness, grief, and abandonment; of rejection; of physical and mental illness; of life without meaning; of boredom and restlessness.

In this chapter, we shall explore the qualities of wilderness, the paradigm *par excellence* of encounter with the Divine. We shall first take a brief look at the way different interpretations of wilderness unfold throughout Scripture; then we shall reflect upon those qualities of wilderness which make it so fitting a place in which to encounter God in all our nakedness and vulnerability. Finally, we shall then explore different types of personal desert experiences where, paradoxically, God may seem so far away yet is present in so profound and effective a manner.

It stands to reason that the journey into union with God would follow the same pattern established thousands of years ago, a pattern traced throughout Scripture from Genesis to Revelation. The journey into the mystery of the Divine invariably follows the same route; the journey into freedom follows the same path trod through countless ages, the path into wilderness and desolation; the path into loneliness and confusion; the path into abandonment; the path which leads to the place where our demons abide, but also the path which leads to safety, the path which leads to freedom, the path which leads to life.

Let us now take a look at the various ways in which Scripture affords to the desert experience life-giving and life-enhancing significance. There are four ways by which we may look upon the desert as the locus of encounter with the Divine and the place through which we are led, always under the gaze of a loving and compassionate God, into closer union with Him. These four ways are (i) wilderness as a place of refuge; (ii) wilderness as a place of liberation; (iii) wilderness as a place of healing and forgiveness; (iv) wilderness as a place where we wrestle with our demons.

(i) Wilderness as a place of refuge

In Genesis, 1 Kings, and 1 Maccabees, the desert was the traditional place of refuge for those who were persecuted, a place where God offers succour and safety. In Genesis, we read how Hagar found new life and promise in the desert when she fled from the wrath of her mistress, Sarah. The wilderness was the setting where the angel of the Lord found her by a spring of water and told her not to be afraid to return to her mistress because one day, she would become mother of a multitude (Gen. 16), not such a bad prospect for an Egyptian slave girl. Some five chapters later, we again find her in the wilderness of Beersheba in the depths of despair, as she watched her son dying of thirst when the water-skin had run dry. The angel of the Lord had deceived her by making her such an empty promise. In that very moment of utter darkness, she experienced for herself and for her son the saving power of God, who caused water to well up in the desert for her child and for herself (Gen. 21).

As we are called into closer union with God, the water-skin of consolation and inner peace so often runs dry, and we move into a place of sterility and barrenness, a place of uncertainty and agitation. It is no accident that the words *aridity* and *dryness* are chosen to describe such feelings. These words are fitting descriptions because they evoke the experience of desolate and parched expanses and waterless tracts where the human spirit encounters the Divine. The movement into the mystery of the Divine feels like anything but movement; we feel stuck, no movement, no sense of the presence of God. Or, as Thomas Hood would have it:

> No warmth, no cheerfulness, no healthful ease,
> No comfortable feel in any member
> No shade, no shine, no butterflies, no bees,
> No fruits, no flowers, no leaves, no birds!
> November![1]

---

[1] *The Poetry of Thomas Hood* (Kindle edition, Portable Poetry, 2013).

As we pray through our November times, sitting physically or metaphorically with clenched teeth and whitened knuckles, wishing to be put out of our misery, all we can do is open ourselves resolutely to whatever appears not to happen, clinging in naked faith to the belief that God knows what He is doing, yet at the same time, we can't help but feel that God has abandoned us.

Elijah experienced such feelings, as mentioned at the beginning of the chapter. It was into the wilderness that Elijah fled from the wrath of Jezebel; the wilderness was to be his grave, for it was there that he lay down and asked that he should die because he no longer had any reason to live. The place of his despair became the place of hope, and the bread prepared by the angel gave him strength to walk for forty days to Horeb, the mountain of God (1K. 19: 3f). God fed Elijah in a barren desert, so does He feed us in our own experiences of wilderness.

Hagar fled into the wilderness to seek refuge from the wrath of Sarah; Israel escaped from the murderous rage of Pharaoh, taking refuge in the wilderness of Sinai; Elijah escaped into the wilderness to escape from the anger of

Jezebel. The desert is not always, however, a place of refuge and safety, as we read in the first book of Maccabees. At the time of the Maccabees, those who refused to obey King Antiochus's edict to sacrifice to idols and profane the Sabbath faced certain death or exile, so those "who were seeking righteousness and justice went down to the wilderness to dwell there" (1 Mc. 2: 29). However, as Scripture recounts, they were pursued by the king's men, and because they refused to take up arms on the Sabbath to defend themselves, they were slaughtered: "So they attacked them on the Sabbath, and they died with their wives and children and cattle, to the number of a thousand persons" (1 Mc. 2:37-39). From this account, we find that God does not always rescue his faithful ones, and the desert becomes a place where they encounter death.

Yet, even so, it is into the desert that the woman "clothed with the sun, with the moon under her feet" fled from the great red dragon in the book of Revelation. The woman "fled into the wilderness where she has a place prepared by God in which to be nourished." (Rev. 12: 1ff). For her, and sometimes for us, our wilderness experiences (which we shall explore further on in the chapter) are places prepared by God where we are to be fed, yet, as we have seen, it is sometimes a place of refuge and safety; it is a place where God may lead to freedom; it is also an arid, featureless place, a desolate place where the desert winds scour the spirit and leave it raw and parched. So the face of wilderness is the face of Janus, pointing in the opposite directions of threat and safety, of freedom and slaughter, and therefore a complex place which sometimes offers refuge from danger but, at other times, offers little security or comfort.

(ii) Wilderness as a place of liberation

The inaugural vision of Moses took place at the west side of the wilderness on Mount Horeb. There he first encountered the presence of the living God in the burning bush (Ex. 3), and there he became the instrument of God's liberating activity, which found its full expression in the wilderness of Sinai, into which God led His chosen people out of slavery, there to make a covenant with His children. For forty years, Israel wandered through the wilderness; it was the abrasiveness of the wind and sand which purified the people from their wilfulness, and it was the desert heat which forged them into the people of God, there to be fed and given to drink by the power of the Lord.

No longer slaves, they were free to respond to the call of their God with willing hearts, and so likewise it is in the wilderness that we find Jeremiah responding in freedom but with a certain measure of reluctance to the call of God. It was in desert wastes that Jeremiah cut his teeth and worked out his apprenticeship as prophet; while still a youth, he sought out a desert place, where he surrendered himself unreservedly to his God: "I remember the devotion of your youth, your love as a bride, how you followed me in the wilderness in a land not sown" (Jer. 2:2). Once again, we are confronted by a paradox in the way God deals with the human spirit. The desert is infertile, "a land not sown" yet it is precisely in the land not sown that the Word of God is sown in the heart of Jeremiah, a seed which was to grow and flourish and bear much fruit. It is only in the silence of desert places and in the silence of our own hearts as we come before God in prayer, that we can hear the voice calling us to prepare the way of the Lord. It is within the emptiness of Mary's womb that the seed of God is sown, the seed which was eventually to sprout and burgeon and bring the possibility for reconciliation and peace to the whole universe. And who is to say that God deals with us any differently?

(iii) Wilderness as a place of healing and forgiveness

Even when Israel broke the covenant and went after foreign gods, it was again into the desert that God called His people. "Therefore, behold, I will allure her, and bring her into the wilderness, and speak tenderly to her" (Hos. 2:14). This is a call to return to beginnings, to reclaim once more the experience of the infancy of Israel; it is a call to make all things new once more and start again. Later on, in chapter 11, Hosea reminds us that we are called, once again, not only to remember a time of infancy but also to recreate, under God, the relationship we enjoyed in that infant state: "When Israel was a child, I loved him and out of Egypt I called my son … it was I who taught Ephraim to walk, I took them up in my arms; but they did not know that I healed them. I led them with the cords of compassion, with the bands of love" (Hos. 11:3-4a).

This movement of return in memory is repeated again and again, a movement which forms the basic thrust of this book, a circular movement which brings us spiralling into the heart of God. Hosea reveals God as the Divine Lover who seduces us and whispers in our ears the message of unbelievable intimacy. The point is that we need to be seduced, persuaded, cajoled, enticed, in order to allow ourselves to be drawn into the desert. It is an extremely unpleasant place to be because it is there, like Jesus, that we face our demons, and we will do practically anything to prevent that from happening. We immerse ourselves in all manner of activities rather than enter the stillness and silence of the divine presence. We engage in acts of charity; we go to church; we support aid agencies with money; we try to be tolerant and forgiving, but we, like Adam and Eve before us, sidestep the need to face our God as we are in all our nakedness. Until we know who we really are, by wrestling with our demons and accepting our flaws of character, we shall never be able to face our God in authenticity of spirit. Because the wilderness strips us of all our securities, all our pretensions, all our posturing, it is precisely here that it becomes possible for the authentic self to emerge, naked before God.

(iv) Wilderness as the place where we wrestle with our demons

The desert is a place where forgiveness and healing takes place, but it comes at a cost. The price of our healing is paid in the coin of willingness to wrestle with our demons. This is graphically demonstrated by the feast of Yom Kippur, which celebrates the ritual of atonement, the feast which brings pardon, reconciliation with God, and peace of soul. It is also the place where the desert demon is encountered. Originally, at the heart of the feast was a ceremony at which one goat was sacrificed to the Lord and a second goat was loaded with the sins of the people and driven out into the wilderness to Azazel, the desert demon (Lv. 16: 10): "The goat shall bear their iniquities upon him to a solitary land and he shall let the goat go in the wilderness" (Lev. 16:22). In this instance, the wilderness becomes the place which swallows up the sins of the people and leaves them renewed and cleansed, but only to the extent that the demon becomes involved and takes possession of the darkness of the human spirit.

It was into the wilderness that the Spirit led Jesus to wrestle with his own demons. This was not just a unique event which tested Jesus in order to prepare Him for His public ministry but an abiding and continuous challenge which He faced throughout the course of His life. I suppose one lesson it teaches is that to take the easy way out never really works. "And the tempter said to him, 'If you are the

Son of God, command these stones to become loaves of bread.' But he answered, 'It is written, 'Man shall not live on bread alone, but by every word that proceeds from the mouth of God''' (Mt. 4:3-4).

Although He didn't turn stones to bread, Jesus fed five thousand in the wilderness with five loaves and a couple of fish. And then what happened? When He revealed Himself as the living bread come down from heaven "many of his disciples drew back and no longer went about with him" (Jn. 6: 66). Facing Jesus was the wilderness of confusion. To feed the hungry is something good and positive, surely? What about human suffering? Does the power of God residing in the heart of Jesus eradicate all hunger and disease from the planet? What about the suffering of the innocent? By becoming human, the Son of God immersed Himself in the temptations of the human condition. The temptation of Jesus mirrors the temptation of every parent, that is, the temptation to rescue, the temptation to alleviate disappointment and pain, rather than allow the child to mature and learn through mistakes. It is so painful to stand by and not intervene when a child is suffering, but that is what the Father does because as painful as it is, it's the only way we learn how to become more fully human, more fully alive.

The arid wastes were the place into which Anthony and the other desert fathers entered in order to wrestle with their demons and where the Christian monastic tradition had its origins and from whence it flowered and extended to cover the face of the earth. Monasticism has its roots in the desert, where Pachomius, the father of monasticism (ca. 292–348 CE), dwelt and where, more than a century later, Anthony (ca. 468–ca. 520) spent most of his life. The account of the life of Anthony, written by Athanasius, "presents a brilliant, victorious hero, who goes forth into the desert to brave the devil undaunted and whose fasting and silence reach God. His prophetic wisdom penetrates the human heart and there performs miracles."[2] The reality, however, was, according to his disciples, somewhat less heroic: "The monks recalled an Anthony who did the impossible to escape temptation, who found himself frequently on the verge of despair, who at times lost the strength to pray,

---

2   J. Gribomont, "Eastern Christianity," In *Christian Spirituality: Origins to the Twelfth Century.* Edited by Bernard McGinn and John Meyendorff, Vol. 16 of *World Spirituality: An Encyclopedic History of the Religious Quest*, (New York: Crossroads, 1985) 93.:

who recognized his total ignorance of the divine subjects and of the Scriptures, and whose supreme value was love towards his neighbour."[3] This second portrait of Anthony bears the mark of authentic desert experience, the nature of which we shall now explore in some depth.

From a brief overview of the four ways which are relevant to an understanding of desert as the locus of encounter with the Divine, it is time to move on to the various qualities of wilderness which we encounter in the challenges of day-to-day living and which we may dismiss as having little to do with our relationship with God. What are, then, these qualities of wilderness which make it such a powerful site of encounter with the divine? Firstly, the wilderness is a setting without definable features, other than rocks, sand, and sky. As such, it blurs boundaries and leads us into places of uncertainty, into places where we find ourselves literally be-wildered, where assumptions disappear, where we are left with nothing but ourselves and God alone. The wilderness is a place in which to experience that insecurity, that bewilderment, where God strips us of the false self we have built up over time and

_____

[3] *Ibid.*

gradually allows a self to emerge which is authentic, grounded, and free. The wilderness then becomes a vast sacred space which gives room for our spirits to grow and expand.

Wilderness gives rise to bewilderment, and to be bewildered is to experience mental confusion, a loss of orientation, a loss of direction or purpose. Encounter with the Divine is often a cause of bewilderment and confusion, as the Scriptures amply demonstrate. At the angel's announcing of the Word becoming flesh, Mary's reply was one of bewilderment: "she was greatly troubled at the saying, 'How shall this be, since I have no husband?' (Lk. 1:29, 34). When Mary visited Elizabeth, the reaction she received was one of surprise and confusion: "And why is this granted to me, that the mother of my Lord should come to me?" (Lk. 1: 43). The hearts of Mary and Joseph were filled with perplexity and bewilderment when they found the missing child in the Temple: "'Son, why have you treated us so? Behold your father and I have been looking for you anxiously" And they did not understand (Lk. 2:48 - 50). Neither did the people of Nazareth understand: "Where did this man get all this? And they took offence in him" (Mt. 13:56-57). Neither did the

Pharisees: "Why does he eat with tax collectors and sinners?" (Mk. 2:16). Neither did Peter: "Lord, do you wash my feet?" (Jn. 13:6). Jesus, as a sign of contradiction, frequently caused confusion among his hearers: "Many who heard him were astonished, saying 'Where did the man get all this? What is the wisdom given to him?... Is not this the carpenter, the son of Mary and brother of James and Joses and Judas and Simon?'" (Mk. 6:2-3).

Confusion reigns when we attempt to limit the Lord within the narrow confines of our own expectations. A sense of bewilderment and confusion teaches us that we cannot domesticate God. Desert confusion and lack of orientation undermine a sense of security and self-assurance. Security and self-assurance, by their very nature, restrict us and blind us to the possibility that things could be different, and not only could be different but must be different if we are to grow and develop. In prayer, we embark on a journey in which the landscape is ever changing. Nothing remains static; nothing remains constant, other than God's abiding love for us and the fondness of His steadfast gaze. It is an unfortunate but necessary part of our spiritual journey that it should lead us (somewhat like the Lord's prediction to Peter in John, 21:18) into places where we would rather not venture.

A second property which the desert possesses is the quality of stillness. When threatened by Pharaoh's advancing chariots, the Israelites complained that it would have been better to serve the Egyptians rather than die in the wilderness. Moses responded with the injunction: "Fear not, stand firm, and see the salvation of the Lord, which he will work for you today, for the Egyptians whom you see today, you shall never see again. The Lord will fight for you, and you have only to be still." (Ex. 14:12-13). "Be still and know that I am God" (Ps. 46:10) is excellent advice for anyone who wishes to grow closer to God, or rather to allow God to grow closer to the self. As I mentioned in the first chapter, Woody Allen's assessment of success was that 80 per cent of success was just turning up. The recipe for a healthy life of prayer is to be present, be quiet, and don't fidget.

Obviously, the early stages of prayer call for the exercise of imagination. In the early stages, we reflect on certain passages in Scripture; we meditate or focus on a particular word or phrase, and repeat it constantly. Even so, prayer time calls for a stillness of body, a letting go of all that stands between us and the Cloud of Forgetting. As we move on, however, we leave everything behind: imagination, focus, mantra, self, and leave everything to God, Who alone works to His own glory and praise. Such was the message God entrusted Isaiah to give to the young King Ahaz: "Take heed, be quiet, do not be afraid" (Is. 7: 4). We have only to be still as is a baby at the mother's breast.

Thirdly, there is an almost tangible quality to the silence of desert spaces. I remember on one occasion driving from Botswana to Zambia through the Kalahari Desert. Along the way, I pulled off the road and got out of the car to stretch my legs. What immediately struck me was the utter silence of the place. I was almost oppressed by the sheer weight of silence, a silence which almost hurt my ears, a silence which was so palpable that it became the speech of God, to which I responded with reverence and awe. Such was the intensity of the experience that it almost reduced me to tears.

Silence and stillness are the indispensable properties of contemplative prayer, and let's face it, we are all called to the prayer of contemplation. "Be still and know that I am God"

(Ps. 46:10) is the precept for all who wish to enter more deeply into a life of prayer, calling for a stilling of intellect, will, and imagination, a self-emptying in the presence of God. When we come to encounter God in prayer, we leave aside our own agenda, our own wishes, our own selves, and enter the desert silence and the desert stillness in order that we more readily hear His voice. "For thus said the Lord God, the Holy One of Israel, 'In returning and rest you shall be saved; in quietness and in trust shall be your strength'" (Is. 30:15).

Once more, we are faced with a paradox: only by embracing stillness that movement can occur. However, the movement happens not of our own volition but by the will of God, bearing us along into the mystery of the Divine, bearing us towards a recapturing and reliving of the world of the small child. As I have repeated so many times, this movement is spiral and draws us more deeply into where we may be more authentic, not only in our relationship with God but also with one another, a movement which leads into a fuller and more vibrant life. We enter into a world of silence, both interior and exterior, a world where we do nothing but waste time gracefully with God.

Silence has value not only in times of formal prayer but also in time of leisure. Perhaps it may promote a more robust prayer life if, on occasion, we switch off the television, radio, iPad, computer or any other source of extraneous noise, just for one evening. Now there's an interesting experiment. As cities and towns suffer from light pollution, which prevents our seeing the glory of the stars at night, so, too, we can equally suffer from noise pollution, where we fail to hear the rustle of leaves on the trees or the birdsong outside the window. Sitting still in silence is, however, not for the faint-hearted. As mentioned above, we can dare to enter such a space only to the extent that we have armed ourselves with living trust and a vibrant hope and are willing to take God at His word. Sitting still in silence exposes us to qualities of wilderness essential for a healthy relationship with God, with neighbour and with our mother earth.

Let's now visit some of the forms which the wilderness can take in our daily lives, forms which at first have little to say about our relationship with God and may be seen, mistakenly, as impediments to spiritual growth. What are the desert experiences we all encounter but often fail to appreciate as opportunities for growth into union? As there are seven gifts of the Spirit, seven virtues, seven deadly sins, there are (for purposes of this chapter, at least) seven forms of wilderness experience: wilderness of darkness of spirit; wilderness of futility; wilderness of loneliness; wilderness of failure; wilderness of loss; wilderness of boredom; wilderness of the tragic.

The Wilderness of Darkness of Spirit

In *Mother Teresa: Come Be My Light,* we are given an insight into the depths of darkness in which Mother Teresa spent most of her adult life. On July 3, 1959, she wrote a letter to Father Picachy in which she included a paper which describes her inner state: In the darkness

> Lord, my God, who am I that You should forsake me? The child of your love and now become as the most hated one, the one You have thrown away as unwanted, unloved. I call, I cling, I want and there is no One to answer, no One on Whom I can cling, No One Alone. The darkness is so dark and I am alone. Unwanted, forsaken. The loneliness of the heart that wants love is unbearable.[4]

---

[4]   Mother Teresa, *Mother Teresa: Come Be My Light*, Edited with commentary by Brian Kolodiejchuk (London, Boston, Sydney, Auckland: Rider, kindle edition, 2008) 186.

Such were the depths of distress and pain in which Mother Teresa found herself that, according to her paper at least, they became an obstacle on her path to union with her God. The fact that she writes in terms of calling, clinging, and wanting indicates that her focus veers away from God towards her own need. She has, however, a precedent in the prayer of Jesus in Gethsemane Who prayed for the chalice of suffering to be taken away, but still He surrendered to the will of His Father. He did not lose His focus, and His prayer was for the will of His Father to be accomplished in His life. Saints, such as Mother Teresa, are only human and make mistakes just like the rest of us and sometimes they provide examples which are not always wise to emulate. At times, however, the inner pain is so intense that it blocks out all other considerations, even the consideration of a God of love.

How may we discern the difference between what is of God and what is of human origin, particularly with regard to the difference between the desolation which comes from God and depression, which does not? In *Dark Night of the Soul,* John of the Cross offers three principal signs by which one may determine if darkness and aridity stem from the work of God or originate from a different source, such as clinical depression or indifference or apathy: The first sign is that if one can take no delight in God or in anything whatsoever, then it is quite probable that a process of purification is taking place. If, however, one takes no delight in God but is quite content to indulge in distractions of whatever sort, then the origin of aridity lies within one's own area of responsibility.

However, if we take this sign to its logical conclusion, we find that it's not particularly helpful because one of the symptoms of a major depressive episode is *anhedonia*, that is, an inability to derive pleasure from anything. One would need to take into consideration the other symptoms of a depressive episode in order to identify the source of strong feelings, such as those Mother Teresa expressed. Symptoms of depression include feeling sad or empty most of the day; significant weight loss or weight gain; disrupted sleep patterns, including early morning wakening; feeling restless and agitated; inability to concentrate; feeling worthless and helpless. If any of these symptoms are present, then it is advisable to seek medical help rather than look upon the suffering these symptoms cause as a cross sent by God to be bravely borne. This is not wilderness; it is depression, pure and simple, which can be treated.

Is it really helpful to make a distinction between desolation and depression? Perhaps it is. In his book *Care of Mind, Care of Spirit*,[5] Gerald May, the American psychiatrist who died in 2005, suggests that if a person's sense of humour, general capacity for functioning, and thoughtfulness towards others remains unimpaired, then it is probably not depression. He states that as he accompanied individuals through the experience of dark night transitions, he never experienced the anger, negativity, and resentment that he encountered when working with people suffering from depression. In his book *The Dark Night of the Soul,* May writes

> This dark night of the soul is a profoundly good thing. It is an ongoing spiritual process in which we are liberated from attachments and compulsions and empowered to live and love more freely. Sometimes this letting go of old ways is painful, occasionally even devastating. But this is not why the night is called "dark." The darkness of the night implies nothing sinister, only that the liberation takes place in hidden ways, beneath our knowledge and understanding. It happens mysteriously, in secret, and beyond our conscious control. For that reason it can be

---

[5] G. May, *Care of Mind, Care of Spirit, (*San Francisco: Harper and Row, 1982) 84-92.

disturbing or even scary, but in the end it always works to our benefit.[6]

The second of John of the Cross's signs is that if one considers oneself to be at fault while attempting to respond to the will of God, then, too, it is probable that the experience is one of purgation for, as John maintains, "it is the nature of lukewarm-ness not to care greatly or to have any inward solicitude for the things of God. There is a great difference between lukewarm-ness and aridity."[7]

The third sign is that one cannot meditate as one did previously, despite intense effort on the part of the soul. Imaginative wanderings no longer fulfil their function and purpose. Instead, they are experienced as hindrances to the movement into the mystery of the Divine. What is happening here, John says, is that God begins to communicate not through sense experience but by "pure spirit ... by an act of simple contemplation, to which neither the exterior nor the interior senses of the lower part of the soul can attain."[8]

---

[6] G. May, *The Dark Night of the Soul: A Psychiatrist Explores the Connection between Darkness and Spiritual Growth* (e-book edition, 2004) 4.

[7] *The Complete Works of St John of the Cross*, Volume 1, Translated and edited by E. Allison Peers,: (The Newman Press, 1953) 352.

[8] *Ibid.* 355.

Simply stated, aridity and darkness are indications of a movement away from discursive meditation into prayer of contemplation. What is happening here is that meditation, which relies partly on human effort, gives way to the prayer of contemplation. Whereas in meditation, God grants consolation and feelings of peace in order that the human spirit be not discouraged, in contemplation, there is the demand for complete detachment from all sense consolation. We are there exclusively so that God may work in the Spirit as and how He judges fit. We come naked into the dark of the spirit; we enter the Cloud of Unknowing and invite God to enter in. The prayer of the dark wilderness is the prayer of Job, robbed of everything: "Naked came I from my mother's womb, and naked shall I return; the Lord gave, and the Lord has taken away; blessed be the name of the Lord" (Job 1:21).

Based on Paul's words that "We know that in everything God works for good with those who love him" (Rm. 8: 28), even the darkness of depression, distressing and debilitating as it may be, also serves as a wilderness where we can encounter the divine. Depression breeds a sense of helplessness, which throws us back into a state of dependency, which we experienced as children; helplessness can lead to an acknowledgement that we cannot go it alone, but literally, in all things, we depend on the help of God. However, to experience depression and not to seek help leaves one in the same state as the man who was hanging from a cliff and refused all offers of help from a helicopter hovering above. The man shouted that God would save him. Finally, he lost his grip and fell to his death. On meeting God at the gates of heaven, he complained bitterly that he had trusted the Lord only to be let down. "Well," said God, "I did send you a helicopter."

The transition from meditative to contemplative prayer invariably is one which involves feelings of being left in the dark without consolation. Don't worry. The dawn will rise again, and one only has to exercise a little patience. This is a time, like all such times of dryness and darkness, where once more, an attitude of patient waiting is vital. This is the stance taken by Simeon and Anna in the Temple of Jerusalem, waiting for the consolation of Israel (Lk. 2: 25). We simply have to wait in the darkness and allow God to love us as He knows best, without consolation, without a sense of inner peace, waiting on Calvary, where there was darkness from

174

the sixth until the ninth hour when the sun refused its light. Would that the darkness lasted only three hours but, for some like Mother Teresa, it can seem to last forever. For whatever its worth, the wilderness of darkness is precisely the locus of connection with God and the place where the mystery of divine healing unfolds, deep within, unfelt, unknown.

The one who sits in the wilderness of darkness and who is faithful to the Absent God in an act of profound love and generosity becomes a portal of grace and healing, not necessarily for herself or for himself but for countless sisters and brothers throughout the world. It is imperative, it is vital that one not abandon prayer because to sit alone in the valley of the shadow of death brings with it the healing of the world.

We are part of such an intricate web of connections that every action, every reaction resonates and reverberates throughout humanity. Paul calls our attention to this fact in his first letter to the Corinthians: "For just as the body is one and has many members, and all the members of the body, though many, are one body, so it is with Christ.... If one member suffers, all suffer together; if one member is honoured all rejoice together" (1 Cor. 12: 12- 26). This applies not only to the baptised but to the whole of creation. The one who dwells in the desert of darkness and makes a self-offering to God in prayer becomes a channel through which the healing grace of the Lord flows and touches the earth, bringing to fulfilment the prophesy of Isaiah: "The wilderness and the dry land shall be glad, the desert shall rejoice and blossom abundantly, and rejoice with joy and singing" (Is. 35:1-2).

The Wilderness of Futility

In the seventies, I worked for a year in a retreat house in Houston, Texas. While giving a clergy retreat, one young priest came and asked if he could have a word with me. We went into the office, and I asked him how I could help. The young man was deeply distressed. He asked me did I know how he was feeling. "Tell me," I said. "I feel like a fireplace," he said. What he was telling me was that here we were, some sixty miles inland from the Gulf of Mexico, where in winter, the temperature rarely dropped sufficiently to warrant lighting a fire. This young priest, ordained a matter of months with the oil of ordination scarcely dry on his hands, full of energy and zeal, thought of himself as ineffectual, having no useful role. Like a fireplace, his function was purely ornamental, something easily overlooked and taken for granted. This indeed placed the young man squarely in the desert of futility. One of the basic human needs is the need to be needed, to matter in someone's life, to know that someone cares whether we live or die.

The desert of futility is a place familiar to elderly residents of a care home. One is thought to be stupid because she is hard of hearing. There she sits, waiting to be brought a cup of lukewarm tea with too much milk; there sits another waiting for her children who never come; there he sits in a quiet rage of frustration, alienating all around him with his bitterness because he can't quite lay hold of the words. What's the use? The barren futile desert of hatred and violence that mars the face of our gentle earth evokes the prayer of the Crucified: "My God, my God, why hast thou forsaken me?" (Mt. 27: 46).

This is the humanity in which we are involved: the girl forcibly abducted from her school and sold into slavery; the child subjected to physical and sexual abuse. Herein lies our diminishment and the helplessness and feelings of futility which we bring to prayer. This is why it is so important to be present to God in prayer. We bring all the suffering of humanity with us; we bring all the joy and love as well.

As well as possessing a passive component, the component which speaks of suffering and powerlessness, futility has also an active part to play in adding to the distress of the human mind. We have an abiding tendency at times to shoot ourselves in the foot. People often engage in futile behaviour patterns to their own detriment and to that of others, even though they know such behaviours are self-destructive and harmful to others. Addictive patterns of behaviour are a case in point. Men and women sometimes overindulge in alcohol in order to diminish the tension caused by stress and anxiety, even though they know that any relief gained is only temporary and that, because alcohol is a central nervous system depressant, that when the temporary relief lifts, the subsequent anxiety and depression is even deeper. Another example is that of a person who attempts to gain attention by inappropriate behaviour, knowing full well that it doesn't work. And to some extent, we are all guilty of that.

In May 1919, Freud began work on his essay *Beyond the Pleasure Principle*. Originally, he thought that all mental life was driven by the pleasure principle, the purpose of which is to diminish unpleasant sensations: a baby is wet; it demands immediate attention; a baby is hungry and makes its needs known in no uncertain terms. Freud writes, "Under the influence of the ego's instincts of self-preservation, the pleasure principle is replaced by the reality principle."[9] Around the age of five, the child gradually becomes aware that other people have needs as well, which not only have to be acknowledged but, in civilised society, must also be honoured. In *Beyond the Pleasure Principle,* Freud introduces the concept of the death instinct, which contrasts with the Eros principle, and at the core of which lies the compulsion to repeat unpleasant and self-defeating behaviours. He cites the instance of a child of eighteen months who invents a game in which he throws a favourite toy out of his crib, reels it back in, and repeats the performance. By so doing, he achieves "the instinctual renunciation which he made in allowing his mother to go away without protesting. At the outset he was in a passive

---

[9] S. Freud, "Beyond the Pleasure Principle" In *Abstracts of the Standard Edition of the Complete Works of Sigmund Freud.* Edited by Carrie Lee Rothgeb (Jason Aaronson, 1987) 204.

situation, but, by repeating it, unpleasurable though it was, as a game, he took on an active part."[10]

Repetitive patterns of thinking and acting become hardwired in the brain and are hard to change. Just think how hard it is to give up smoking, to stop biting one's nails, or to stop fiddling with one's hair, and how hard it is for someone to change addictive behaviour. People tend to make the same mistakes over and over, such as breaking up with an abusive partner, only to repeat the mistake by getting involved with someone else who is equally abusive. The compulsion to repeat forms an obstacle on the path to freedom, and prayer brings with it an antidote in that it shines a light on our foibles and brings us to a greater depth of self-awareness, giving us insight into how we may change. Conversion is, as we have seen, a permanent process, an engagement of a lifetime.

Our compulsions and drives speak to the wilderness of futility which we bring to prayer because we can never leave ourselves outside the door. When we come to prayer, we bring with us not only our own wilderness but that of the whole of created reality. Given the intricate web of connections

_____

[10] *Ibid.*

which link us, not only to other human beings, not only to all other living things, but to the whole of creation, animate and inanimate, we bring not only our own sense of futility but that of all created reality. We bring the futility of war and famine; we bring the futility of domestic violence; we bring the futility of the ravaging of our mother earth. The litany of distress is practically endless, and the only thing that allows us to enter the desert of futility with any sense of acceptance, if not tranquillity, is the belief and hope that all that is, lies in the hands of God, and that at some time in the future, "all will be well."

Allied to a sense of futility is the sense of frustration. Habakkuk prays to God, "O Lord how long shall I cry for help, and thou wilt not hear? Or cry to thee 'Violence!' and thou wilt not save? Why dost thou make me see wrongs and look upon trouble?" (Hab. 1:2-3). Or our prayer may be that of Psalm 13: "How long O Lord? Wilt thou forget me forever? How long wilt thou hide thy face from me? How long must I bear pain in my soul, and have sorrow in my heart all the day?"

Frustration emerges when we are prevented from achieving a set goal. This is why it is so vitally important when we come to prayer not to bring with us our own agenda because if we do, then we are doomed to experience frustration. If we become frustrated with God because He is not listening or responding the way we expect, then it is very tempting to abandon prayer. Or we regress to childhood patterns of behaviour and metaphorically stamp our foot and shout, "I don't care!"

In a wider context, frustration can, according to some research, lead to aggression, and when satisfaction cannot be obtained by addressing the source of frustration (unemployment; political ineptitude; abuse of power; unequal access to resources), then there is a tendency to scapegoat a section of the population: immigrants, illegal or legal; Muslims; gays and lesbians; any minority group which does not possess the political or economic clout to stand up for itself. This is the world in which we live; this is the world we bring with us before God in prayer. This is the desert experience of wilderness, frustration, darkness of spirit.

And sometimes, our prayer is that of John Henry Newman, who, when he was becalmed on an orange boat (a boat transporting oranges, not one which was painted orange) for a week in the Straits of Bonifacio, penned the words of the hymn "Lead Kindly Light". Perhaps, like Newman, when we find ourselves in the arid desert of darkness, frustration, and confusion, all we can dare ask for is not to see the distant scene but for just sufficient light to see one step ahead.

The Wilderness of Loneliness

When I returned to England from working in South Africa, I was asked to serve in a parish in north London. The counter-cultural shock was far worse than anything I had ever previously experienced. It was a time of intense loneliness, of adjusting to the fact that I was no longer able to serve the people of the African township of Khutsong, the people I had come to know and love so well. The acceptance with which the African villagers received me contrasted starkly with the indifference of a large urban population. With longing in my heart, I prayed, asking God to send someone to give me a hug. That's all. I didn't want the earth, only a hug. Such was my prayer, which went on for months. During my work there, I came to know the members of the folk group who provided the music for Sunday's midday Mass. One morning, as I was preparing for the midday Mass, one of the folk group came into the sacristy and asked to have a word. I asked him if it could wait until after Mass, as there wasn't much time. He said that it would only take a minute, so I asked him how I might help. He then told me that he had finally decided to inform his parents that he was gay, having agonised over the decision for some time. I gently congratulated him for his courage and honesty, and told him that we would speak at greater length later. He turned to leave, and as he reached the sacristy door, he turned around, came back to me and said, "David, would you please give me a hug?" Such is the way of God.

Loneliness can be so corrosive because it diminishes one's sense of self-worth, which leads to a conviction that we are nothing in the sight of God and there is little purpose to life. It doesn't necessarily depend on being isolated or alone and can be felt even when one has family and friends. Loneliness may be a response to a change in life circumstances: moving away from family and friends; taking on a new job; an unhappy or failed marriage; having a baby; retirement; being misunderstood; or having one's motives questioned. Forlorn feelings may stem from a mental disorder, such as acute anxiety or clinical depression, or may stem from social isolation. Irrespective of the cause, loneliness can have an adverse impact on our sense of self and our relationship with God. If I feel important to no one, then feelings automatically arise that I am also unimportant to God, and I project my feelings onto Him. On the other hand, loneliness may have a positive outcome, in that it may contribute to a greater fidelity to prayer. If I feel that I have nobody, then at least I have God.

It is always tempting to act out our feelings; the stronger the feelings the greater is the drive to act on them. Equally seductive is the temptation to use the way we feel as a barometer of our standing with God. Time and time again, when working with individuals who wish to develop their spiritual life, I have to emphasise the truth that feelings are no measure by which to gauge where we stand before God, and if we base our understanding of our relationship with God upon the way we feel, then we are seriously deluding ourselves. And if we adopt a primitive way of thinking, we are in danger of locking ourselves out of the possibilities for growth.

Loneliness is a natural by-product of spiritual growth. This loneliness is due to no one else understanding, appreciating, or sharing the depth of longing, the raging thirst for the things of God. It's exquisitely isolating to have no one you can share your life of prayer with. Speaking of such matters renders you liable to be thought a bit peculiar, a little unbalanced. So you remain silent about what is the most significant, the most important, the most vital concern in your life; you may experience profound loneliness and isolation as a result. This is truly a wilderness from which there seems to be no way out. But that's all right because it is the voice of God which seduces and leads you father into the desert, where the Lord will whisper to your heart. Being open to loneliness leads to a radical awareness of our complete dependence on God which, in turn, leads to a reverence and respect for all that is. This brings with it the acknowledgement that we are part of all that is and that we are come alone into the world and that we are going to depart in exactly the same way.

The Wilderness of Failure

Just a cursory glance at Paul's second missionary journey reveals the number and extent of failures that he suffered. His second missionary journey began when he had a violent disagreement with Barnabas over John Mark and refused to take him with him, so he and Barnabas went their separate ways (Acts 15: 36ff). At Philippi, he and Silas were beaten with rods because, in a fit of irritation, Paul had exorcised a slave girl and rendered her useless to her owners, who had made money from her ability to foretell the future (Acts 16: 16ff). Coming to Thessalonika, Paul and Silas fell foul of the Jews, and the brethren had to send them away secretly by night (Acts 17: 10). The Jews heard that Paul was at Beroea, and they followed him there and stirred up trouble so that he was forced to depart, leaving Silas and Timothy behind (Acts 17: 13). He was then taken to Athens, where he tried to engage the philosophers who, with a contemptuous sneer, demanded, "What would this babbler say?" (Acts 17: 18), They led him to the Areopagus, where he was mocked for his preaching on the resurrection.

Yet again, Paul encountered failure. His trusted companions were no longer with him. If he failed in Athens, what chance would he ever have in Corinth, which was to be his next port of call? As a seaport town, with a string of brothels along the waterfront, Corinth was a place of loose morals, where the very word Corinthian meant a depraved and licentious person. How on earth was Paul going to succeed in planting the seed of Good News if he had been such an abject failure in the sophistication and culture of Athens?

In reflecting on his experience, Paul sensed the familiarity with a pattern of long ago. Yes, God had brought triumph out of failure; the Lord had brought life out of death; He had created new beginnings out of old endings. If this is how the Father dealt with the Son, then Paul, conforming to the pattern of the death of Jesus, as he himself writes, would become a vessel of the life of God, bringing His saving act to birth in the hearts of the people of Corinth, not through his strength but through his weakness, not through his success, but through his failure.

On a personal note, my most painful experience of failure occurred in the early 1980s. In 1981, I was appointed as director of a retreat house and Rector of the community. In June 1983, I was relieved of my post by the provincial, who gave me no reason for doing so. I later learned that he had received complaints from members of the community, the nature of which were never shared with me. I was devastated, and the blow to my self-confidence was enormous. The provincial wanted to send me to Australia, like some disgraced criminal of old. However, the Australian provincial would not accept me. I was left in some sort of limbo, which felt more like hell. The following month, I went over to Ireland to give a retreat. Before the retreat, I stayed in our house in Dublin, where I had studied before ordination. One morning, on leaving my room, I met a priest who had taught me during my student days. We chatted, and I asked him what he was doing. He told me that he was about to go to the United States to train as a spiritual director. At that instant a light came on in my head because this was something I had always wanted to do. He promised that he would leave all the information at my door. I went downstairs for coffee and met the Irish provincial, who invited me into his office for a chat. He asked what I was doing, and I told him I was doing absolutely nothing. He then told me he was desperate to have someone help in a parish in South Africa; would I be willing to help out? These two encounters changed my life completely, and had it not been for the fact that I had been relieved of my post, I would not have moved into areas of life which have enriched me immeasurably. Neither would I have had cause, on such a deep and personal level, to reflect on the mystery of the failure of Christ and the darkness of Gethsemane. In prayer and reflection, I came to understand that this is the way God works, bringing hope out of despair; bringing light out of darkness; bringing success out of failure; bringing life out of death.

The Wilderness of Loss

It is all very well for Luke to tell stories of a lost sheep, or a coin, or even a lost child because in each instance, they are found and restored. What happens when what is lost remains lost forever? Some losses are life-changing, and we are inconsolable because what has been lost is never restored. Many and varied are the losses we experience as we go through life, yet each occurs under the compassionate gaze of God. Each year, as Christmas approaches, we buy cards and go through the address book, crossing out the names of those who have died since last Christmas, names of those to whom we'll never again send greetings.

From the moment we are born, we are subjected to the experience of loss. For nine months as we nestled in the womb, we were warm and safe, protected against the encroachments of sound, light, and temperature, constantly fed. There were no pangs of hunger, no assault on our senses. Then, we were thrust into an alien world where we experienced an almost unbearable invasion of sense experiences upon our eyes and ears, suffering the indignity of being manhandled and slapped; and to add insult to injury, with a snip, we lost connection with the one who protected us all through our gestation. No longer physically connected, we experienced profound isolation, profound loss. But nature is marvellous: Our screams of protest, our cries of rage opened our lungs, and so we took our first breath and, by so doing, began to live a new life. Without the experience of loss, we would never have registered our protest in so vocal a manner, and so it is that the very experience of loss enabled us to live. Perhaps in the same way, successive experiences of loss open up the possibility of attaining life on a deeper level.

One of the abiding tragedies of loss is the fact that it is cumulative: subsequent losses resonate with and amplify earlier losses. No loss is trivial; each in its own way is devastating, and each loss sustained builds upon the other. There is a rhyme which enjoys a long history dating back to the Middle Ages, a verse Ben Franklin included in his *Poor Richard's Almanack*:

> For want of a nail the shoe was lost.
> For want of a shoe the horse was lost.
> For want of a horse the rider was lost.
> For want of a rider the message was lost.
> For want of a message the battle was lost.
> For want of a battle the kingdom was lost.
> And all for the want of a horseshoe nail.[11]

One of the more poignant expressions of loss in Scripture is David's lament over the death of his third son, Absalom, who had risen up in revolt against his father. Absalom was killed by Joab, and when the news of his death was brought to the king, David wept bitterly: "And the king was deeply moved, and went up to the chamber over the gate, and wept; and as he went, he said, 'O my son Absalom, my son, my son Absalom! Would I had died instead of you. O Absalom, my son, my son!'" (2 Sam. 19:1 JB). Perhaps there is no loss as painful as the death of a child because it involves so many

---

[11] B.Franklin, *Poor Richard's Almanack,* (June 1758, facsimile ed., vol. 2) 375, 377.

different feelings: raw grief; disbelief; guilt that perhaps more could have been done to save the child's life; bitterness at the unfairness of life; resentment of other parents with healthy children. How does one come before God in prayer and resist the temptation to blame Him and to question His loving-kindness? How can one possibly accept what is totally unacceptable? The terrible wilderness of loss consumes everything and has the potential to alienate the spirit from God. There is little consolation to be had except in the faith to believe that God weeps along with the grieving parent, in silence, because no words can adequately express sympathy for such pain.

The subjective experience of loss is grief and grief is a feeling of profound emptiness and longing. The human spirit is scoured by the abrasive winds of grief; not only scoured but expanded, widened, deepened. The wombs of the women of Scripture were barren, quickened only by the power of God; the womb of Mary became the vessel of containment for the Word precisely because it was empty, open to the vivifying power of the Spirit, who looked with favour on the emptiness of the handmaid of the Lord. The Spirit fills the empty with good things and sends the rich away with nothing. It is only to the extent that a flute is hollow that it can make music; we are instruments, fashioned by the loving hand of God, who make celestial music to delight the ear, but only when we are sufficiently empty to allow the breath of God to blow gently through us. And loss and grief are instruments of emptiness, powerlessness, and dependence.

Loss comes in all shapes and sizes, one of which is loss through separation. Such was the case when Paul said good-bye to the elders at Ephesus for the last time: "And when he had spoken thus, he knelt down and prayed with them all. And they all wept and embraced Paul and kissed him, sorrowing most of all because of the word he had spoken, that they should see his face no more" (Acts 20: 36-38). Saying a final good-bye to a precious friend is indeed an experience of wilderness. The desert of futility, the wilder-ness of loneliness, pale in comparison to the wilderness of loss.

Yet, it is the generous willingness to abide deep within the wilderness of loss which defines the disciple. In the tenth chapter of Matthew's Gospel, and in parallels in the other synoptic Gospels, there is a radical call to renunciation: Those who love father or mother more than the Lord are not worthy of Him; those who love son or daughter more are not worthy of Him. The renunciation is so radical that it demands the renunciation of the very self: "He who does not take his cross and follow me is not worthy of me. He who finds his life will lose it, and he who loses his life for my sake will find it" (Mt. 10:34-39). Sometimes, all we have to cling to in prayer is the promise of Jesus in His Eucharistic discourse: "I will not leave you desolate; I will come to you" (Jn. 14:18). He comes with the promised Spirit as Counsellor, Consoler and Advocate. He comes to remind us that, most especially in moments of tragedy and darkness, we live and move and have our being under the gentle gaze of God.

Loss becomes one of the radical experiences of our relationship with the Lord, when we surrender ourselves to that self-emptying which disposes us to receive the fullness of God. The fullness of God's love cannot be gained if we are full of ourselves, independent, and in need of nothing. As God breaks open the shell of Zechariah's complacency when he is struck dumb (Lk. 1: 20), so does He allow the losses we suffer to loosen our chains of self-sufficiency. The Lord always seeks out those who are lost; He leaves the ninety-nine sheep alone while He goes looking for the one which is lost; the woman sweeps all through the house, looking for the lost coin; the father rushes out to meet the son who was lost but is on his way home. What the experience of loss does, as noted in the previous chapter, is to focus our attention and to lead us to reassess our priorities; all other considerations get swept aside while we concentrate on finding the lost wallet, the missing car keys. And so it is with God. Nothing perhaps concentrates the gaze of God quite so much as the floundering of His children. And we may be consoled with the words of St Teresa of Avila in her poem, *When the Holy Thaws* "And God is always there, if you feel wounded. He kneels over the earth like a divine physician and His love thaws the holy in us."[12]

The Wilderness of Boredom

If the colour of the wilderness of loss is black, then the colour of the wilderness of boredom would be anaemic beige. Ennui, tedium, and restlessness are all part of the human condition, attested to by the wisdom literature in the OT,

---

[12] In D. Ladinsky, *Love Poems from God*, (Penguin Compass, 2002) 291.

which simply bristles with warnings against the creeping effects of boredom, sloth, or *acedie,* and is counted among the seven deadly sins. In Proverbs 19:24, there is a graphic and humorous picture of a man eating from the common bowl: "The sluggard buries his hand in the dish, and will not even bring it back to his mouth." The author is apparently so taken with this image that he repeats it five chapters later: "The sluggard buries his hand in the dish; it wears him out to bring it back to his mouth" (Prov. 26: 15). In the fifth century, John Cassian, a disciple of St John Chrysostom, wrote in *Remedies to the Eight Principal Faults,* Book X: "The Spirit of Accidie [is something] which we may term weariness or distress of heart."[13] Sloth was, for Cassian, something particularly distressing to the monk dwelling in the desert in the heat of the midday sun, when the overwhelming temptation was to take an extended siesta, a temptation Cassian compares to "the destruction that wastes at noonday" (Ps. 91: 6).

There are, according to Cassian, two forms of temptation associated with boredom, listlessness, and lack of interest in

---

[13] J. Cassian, *The Twelve Books of John Cassian on the Institutes of the Coeobia and the Remedies for the Eight Principal Faults,* Translated by Rev Edgar C.S. Gibson, (Veritas Splendor Publications, 2012 Kindle edition).

things of the spirit: One is for the monk to remain in his cell and neglect both work and prayer; the other is to go off into the city, seeking distractions under the pretext of visiting the sick or comforting the dying. This second form of temptation is particularly common nowadays. Who has not heard that "the devil makes work for idle hands"? Chapter 48 of the Rule of St Benedict (of the Daily Work) begins with the reflection that idleness is the enemy of the soul. As a novice, I spent my evening recreation period making rosary beads or sandals or birettas; we had to be doing something other than relaxing. It was unthinkable that we should waste time, a notion which was hardly an effective way of preparing us for a life of contemplative prayer. Waste time with God? Heaven forbid. The order of the day was to pray as if everything depends on God and work as if everything depends on us.

Everything, as we know but don't always act upon, does depend on God and on Him alone. Many people feel guilty if they are not doing something, raised as they have been on the idea of the importance of being useful and productive members of society. Rather than spend time idly with God, the temptation is to engage in good works in the name of the Lord, thus sparing oneself from the sometimes tedious pursuit of spending time with God. Far better to be engaged in productive activity and, there is ample justification in Scripture for adopting such an approach: "Through sloth the roof sinks in and through indolence the house leaks" (Ecc.10: 18). The parable of the talents, where industriousness is rewarded and inactivity is condemned, presents a picture of a God who favours venture capitalists over squirrels. Even the last judgement is based on corporal works of mercy.

What makes the temptation to replace prayer with "good works", so insidious, so alluring, is that it allows us to be in control. Once more, we are in the driving seat, and we can feel useful, just as Peter did in chapter 2. He was told to wait, but he couldn't wait; he fished all night and caught nothing. When will we ever learn to trust God? All activity has to flow from prayer, not the other way round. All good works come to nothing if they are not rooted in prayer. We need to take to heart the wisdom of the psalms if our activity is to be fruitful: "Unless the Lord builds the house, those who build it labour in vain. Unless the Lord watches over the city, the watchman stays awake in vain. It is in vain that you rise up early and go late to rest, eating the bread of anxious toil; for he gives to his beloved sleep" (Ps. 127.1-2).

Boredom is not always to be associated with sloth. Sometimes, it implies a general dissatisfaction with life, with relationships which have lost their sparkle. It implies a lack of interest in activities and a disinclination to stir oneself. Doing the same old thing day after day, meeting the same boring people and attending church services, (especially for many youngsters) is boring. Sometimes life is vanilla, not strawberry, and seasons of restlessness and lack of interest are transient. Time and time again, I repeat that we come to prayer as we are, not as we would like to be; we are accepted just as we are, including the times when we are bored and listless. To interpret these feelings as part of life without allowing the feelings to dominate or dictate how we respond to the graceful invitation of God is a mature and healthy way of dealing with the unpleasant, restless feelings of boredom. We don't pray in order to get something out of it; we pray in order to give God praise and thanksgiving, and we pray in order that God may do with us whatever He will.

The Wilderness of the Tragic

Perhaps now is the time to explore the singularly most unsettling desert experience our very humanness subjects us to. In the first chapter of his confessions, Augustine writes, "You have formed us for yourself and our hearts are restless till they find rest in Thee." This restlessness lies deeply embedded in human nature, consisting in the struggle to reconcile the demands of the false self with those of the true self. In the introduction, I made reference to Gustavo Gutierrez and his book *A Theology of Liberation,* where he writes of conversion as "a permanent process in which the obstacles we meet make us seem to lose all we have gained thus far and start again."

Perhaps of all the obstacles we encounter on our journey through life, the greatest is the self, not, I hasten to add, the true, authentic self created in the image and likeness of God but the false self, the public face we present to the world, a self which does not reflect the face of the Lord. We erect a false self as a means of self-protection, an inauthentic screen behind which we hide to protect our vulnerability. We experience a profound need to protect ourselves because, at some level, we are aware of a conflict which resides at the core of our being, a conflict which defines each human person, a basic flaw in the structure of human nature, irrespective of culture, race, or background. To complicate matters even further, there is yet another conflict to face. Within the human heart lies an ache and a yearning which cannot fully be assuaged because there exists an inescapable conflict between human limitations and the hardwired determination to transcend those limits, The reality of this conflict brings us face to face with the tragic dimension of human existence, the tragic face of human becoming which touches upon four areas of human desire and which can either make us or break us as we move into the mystery of the Divine.

The first domain where we encounter the tragic is in the irreconcilable conflict between the need for separation and the need for merger. We are social beings and, as such, possess a basic impulse to form relationships with others. But the very drive which impels us towards establishing contact with the other, the thrust towards union, at the same time necessarily defeats its own purpose. The reason for this is because the force which operates as an impulse in search of relationship, the expression of a basic need for merger and union, is, equally a drive that impels in the opposite direction towards separation and autonomy. This is because nature has endowed us, like the rest of the animal kingdom, with an instinct for self-preservation, one which protects us from loss of self through absorption in the other, the instinct which protects us against the fear of annihilation. This is what makes the journey into union with God so difficult at times and so problematic.

Freud reminds us in his essay *The Economic Problem of Masochism* that the psychological growth of the child demands an ever-increasing detachment from parents. The act of separation lies at the very beginning of extra-uterine life with the cutting of the umbilical cord. The self that wishes to be merged with the other, in other words, to recapture what Freud calls "a state of oceanic bliss," can never be recaptured because there is the constant pull in the opposite direction towards autonomy and independence. Desire is at continuous odds with need, and the conflict engendered between desire and need forms the root of the tragic dimension of what it means to be human. Awareness, on the baby's part, of no longer being merged, losing forever the sense of harmony with the mother, having the myth of one's omnipotence shattered, further opens the infant to an awareness of isolation, limitation, and loss, an experience upon which the story of banishment from Eden is based.

A second area, similar to the first, where we encounter the tragic is found in the conflict between the opposing needs to be safely held and the need to be free, the need for certainty and security on the one hand, and the need to struggle against being contained and restricted on the other. There is the desire to keep to the safety and familiarity of home and, at the same time, a practically incurable itch to discover what lies on the other side of the mountain. Marjorie Hewitt Suchocki calls this the tension between freedom and finitude.[14] On the one hand, there is need for containment, and on the other, a need for independence. The struggle starts early in life, with a constant need for secure holding within the circle of the mother's arms and later within expanding circles of containment of home and school. Without such secure holding, the infant and child are in constant terror of being dropped, a state of panic which Winnicott describes as a fear of falling forever. However, the

---

[14] M.H. Suchocki, *The End of Evil: Process Eschatology in Historical Context,* (Albany: State University of New York Press, 1988).

very thing which contains, the very thing which provides a boundary, hence a zone of safety, is also that which sets a limit to human possibility and human discovery. Human beings are blessed, or cursed, with the inborn need to transcend limits, to be as gods, but at the same time, they are possessed by a need for a containing boundary, without which they become exposed to the terror of infinite falling. The desire to transcend limits is part of human nature, and if the limits are too rigid and constricting, then what in the best of circumstances is a healthy container becomes instead a suffocating and restrictive enclosure which imprisons the human spirit.

A third area of human desire where we meet the tragic is also similar to the first and consists in the desire, invariably doomed to failure, to possess the other. It is this very quality of otherness after which we lust because it is the one quality that we do not ourselves possess. Awareness that someone else has something we do not have can breed envy, acquisitiveness, and a desire to possess. But we cannot possess, we cannot incorporate the other, for if we could do so, then the very quality of otherness that we so covet would cease to exist in the act of being possessed. Ceasing to exist, it would cease to be an object of desire, but its memory would leave us nonetheless with feelings of frustration and incompleteness. Otherness stands as a perpetual reminder of our basic isolation, mocking our futile aspirations to possess, turning our desires to ashes in our mouths.

In *The Psychoanalytic Vocation: Rank, Winnicott and the Legacy of Freud,* Peter Rudnytsky cites Marion Milner, who in her characteristically graphic way offers us the example of a cannibal to illustrate this point: "The cannibal may be prompted to eat his enemy by love for his courage and strength and wish to preserve these, but it is a love which certainly does not preserve the loved enemy in his original form."[15] She goes on to add "that what one loves most, because one needs it most, is necessarily separate from oneself; and yet the primitive urge of loving is to make what one loves part of oneself. So that in loving it one has, in one's primitive wish, destroyed it as something separate and outside and having an identity of its own."[16]

---

[15] P.Rudnytsky, *The Psychoanalytic Vocation: Rank, Winnicott and the Legacy of Freud* (New Haven: Yale University Press, 1991) 106.
[16] *Ibid.*

A fourth area of human desire where we encounter the tragic lies in the fusion between human destructiveness and creativity, more particularly, in the impossibility of separating out the destructive from the creative impulse. It is this element of the tragic which lies beneath the poet Rilke's decision to abandon psychotherapy. Rilke feared, as mentioned earlier, that if therapy were to exorcise his own personal demons, then his angels would also depart. Frieda Frey-Rohn asserts that creativity "is at the same time both productive and destructive"[17] because something new comes to light only with the destruction of the old. The infant can come to exist as an independent self only through the psychic repudiation and destruction of the other. The only way that the self can emerge is to rise phoenix-like out of the ashes of the psychological merger with the mother. This is the struggle facing many a teenager when subject to the powerful forces of movement away from dependence towards autonomy, towards establishing individuality; it is a struggle which frequently can cause painful conflict with the parents.

---

[17] H. Frey-Rohn, "Evil from the Psychological Point of View", in *Evil*: *Curatorium of the C.G. Jung Institute of Zurich* (Evanston, Ilinois: Northwestern University Press, 1967) 188.

Coming to terms with what it means to be human confronts us with the inalienable and intrinsic character of humanness, namely, its incompleteness. There is an essential pathos to the human condition in that part of us is broken and fragmented. Consequently, we shield ourselves from the disconnectedness of our very being by erecting a false self which, at the same time, prevents the true self from emerging into freedom. The false self has to be abandoned if we wish to stand before God with any claim to authenticity.

Small children at Christmas sometimes prefer to play with a present's gift wrapping rather than enjoy the actual toy. This is a source of puzzlement to parents, who wonder why they went to the trouble and expense of buying the present in the first place. The false self is the wrapping paper which conceals the true self, lying hidden beneath. The wilderness of the tragic gives the opportunity for God at least to loosen the wrapping paper, if not remove it altogether. But, and it is a big but, we have to allow God to do so, which, is no easy matter, as we all know.

The wilderness is a terrible place, a place of pain and darkness. The desert sands scour the spirit in an act of cleansing; (a topic we shall return to in the next chapter). Suffice it to say at present that, in the words of the psalm "Even the darkness is not dark to thee, the night is bright as the day; for darkness is as light with thee" (Ps. 139: 12). For the Lord, darkness is light, and the kindly light by which we are led through these personal desert experiences is the light of the gentle gaze of God, Who loves us so passionately. "For the Lord will comfort Zion; he will comfort all her waste places and will make her wilderness like Eden, her desert like the gardens of the Lord; joy and gladness will be found in her, thanksgiving and the voice of song" (Is. 51: 3).

In this chapter, we have ventured into some painful areas of human becoming. We have explored some of those thorny patches of human endurance, visiting such places as darkness, futility, loneliness, loss and boredom, seeing these places as loci of an encounter with the Divine. As individuals, we follow the same path trodden by the children of Israel. We have found that these desert wastes are not only a place of purification and cleansing but also places of refuge. We take refuge from our demons; we take refuge from our compulsions; we take refuge, most importantly of all, from the false self which we have constructed in the course of our lives.

The desert is where the deceptions of the false self are laid bare. Such deceptions include the idea that you wouldn't like me if you really knew what I'm like. They also include the conventional self; the polite self; the wishing to be thought well of self, but they are all based on unreal self-assessments, and what's even more damning is the realisation that they are focused on a self which is unreal. Being focused on a self lacking a foundation in reality condemns one to a state which lacks authenticity and freedom. Being focused on self means not being focused on God, and as a result, one loses the way. The desert winds strip away the false self, allowing the authentic self to emerge. This self has no interest in whether it is liked, accepted, valued, or not. Its eyes remain on the face of God, and nothing else matters. The wilderness is the place where we are stripped of our illusions, where we stand naked before the gaze of God.

Each and every experience of wilderness changes us and alters the way we relate to God and to the whole of created reality. The epigraph at the head of this chapter reminds us that we cannot undergo experiences of wilderness without emerging from those experiences bearing the imprint of the desert, without being sealed with the stamp that brands the nomad. We carry with us the scars of what we have suffered and, because we are one in Christ, these scars possess the same healing properties as His wounds. By His wounds, we are healed; by our wounds, the whole of the universe is healed. No tear goes unnoticed; no pain is suffered without bearing fruit; no loss is sustained without achieving the healing of the world.

In the next chapter, we shall encounter the effects of the gaze of God, under which we live, move, and have our being. It has been under the gracious gaze of God that we have travelled so far on our journey into the mystery of the Divine; it is under the gaze of God that we shall proceed on our journey into life and love without end; so it is that we shall explore those dimensions of God's gaze which John of the Cross outlines in his Spiritual Canticle. From the sterility and aridity of our desert experiences, God leads us onwards into union with Himself. As the flowers and fruits of the earth draw life from the warmth and light of the sun, so do we draw life and hope from the radiance of God's love for us and His love for all that is.

The following chapter will explore the four blessings which, according to John of the Cross, God works in the human spirit. It is the gaze of God which cleanses us and the whole of the universe; it is the gaze of God which makes us beautiful; and makes us sensitive to the beauty of all that is; it is the gaze of God which enriches and enlightens the face of the earth. It is so incredibly majestic and awesome that we can scarcely believe it; it seems too good to be true. At the same time, the whole process of movement into the mystery of the Divine is so very simple. All it takes, all we have to do, is to be there to let it happen.

Chapter 5

The Fifth Perspective
Under the Gaze of God

This is me, a sinner on whom the Lord has turned his gaze.
Pope Francis, on his election to the papacy.

Beauty is life when life unveils her holy face.
Kahlil Gibran

As a child at school, I was an indifferent student, neither graced with academic ability nor endowed with athletic skills. Vividly I remember the very first lesson in grammar school, when the teacher gave us a pep talk and alerted us that some would benefit greatly from the years of education, while others would drift through school and leave no trace at their passing. I knew then, deep within, that when he spoke of drifters, he was referring to me. I believed that I belonged firmly in the second category, and this belief became a self-fulfilling prophesy. One of the few lessons, the memory of which I did bring with me when I left, was that of an early chemistry lesson, a lesson I remember after all these years because it awoke within me a dawning appreciation of the mystery of life, a mystery of the unfathomable depths of all created reality at the core of which is firelight, the primal source of energy and the life force of all that is. From tiny acorns mighty oaks do grow, and the tiny acorn planted within my spirit by that chemistry lesson was eventually to set me on a journey into that enchantment which resides at the heart of nature, that awe-inspiring enchantment which is the seducing power of God's call into intimacy

All this probably sounds more than a little grandiloquent; however, I make no apology because the truth is, although I couldn't articulate it at the time, my quest was to attain enlightenment from God and, if it be in accordance with His will, ultimately to achieve union with Him. Enlightenment is the reflection within the soul of the light of the gaze of God. Enlightenment is the gaining of new sight/insight into the mystery of the universe; it engenders the capacity literally to see beyond the narrow confines imposed by our spiritual myopia. But enlightenment comes at a cost. Little did I realise the cost to be paid; little did I appreciate the profoundly painful paradox at the heart of the scriptural injunction: One must lose one's life in order to find it. I later discovered that the price of attaining harmony with creation and, more importantly, attaining union with God is paid, more often than not, in the coinage of pain and distress, of sorrow and darkness, for the quest I embarked on and the corresponding longing for union were eventually to immerse me in a sea of utter loneliness and desolation.

Then it came to me! The movement into union with God has to replicate the movement of the Son back to the Father, a movement that entails darkness and suffering, which finds its most profound expression on the cross, with its cry of desolation and abandonment. And the journey still goes on. Today, that desolation is lived in a consciousness of being one with the refugee and the alien one with the young man wrapped in newspaper, huddled in a shop doorway in the depths of a winter's night; one with the young girl trafficked into a life of prostitution. Desolation is experienced in the powerlessness to do little to prevent the rape of the planet. There on the cross of human misery, on the cross of a suffering mother earth, is your God. There is the gateway, such a narrow gateway, into life. The positive slant I have thus far put on our journey into the mystery of the Divine must not blind us to the fact that our footsteps into the Kingdom must frequently follow a path of pain and darkness. In contemplating the Passion of Jesus, I was made aware that the journey into union with God is not for the faint-hearted. Narrow indeed is the doorway into life.

One of the major difficulties in committing oneself to such a journey is that it leads into largely uncharted territories, where one's passing leaves barely a trace. It is also isolating, in that one acquires a world view, a vision into the nature of all that is, much at odds with the predominant world view of commerce, politics, and popular culture. The quest for God entails adopting an alienating view because it involves learning to speak a language largely incomprehensible to those who hear but have not yet acquired the ability to listen with the heart to the music of the universe.

Paradoxically, I also came to understand that light shines in darkness, and the light is the life of all that is. In that early chemistry lesson, I learned that all life depends on a process by which living organisms convert light energy into chemical energy, a process which brings together into a connected whole all living matter through the energy and power of light, a process called photosynthesis. The way the teacher demonstrated the process, in that chemistry lesson, was by taping a coin to the leaf of a plant. The following week, we huddled around his bench as he removed the coin and revealed the dead, grey circle that lay beneath. Without light, there is no life; without the light of God's gaze, we, too, would shrivel and die. We are held in being by the luminosity of God's eternal gaze. Light is the origin of creation; light is the life force which, under God, permeates the universe, holding in being all that is.

Some 14 billion years ago, a fireball erupted, containing within itself the seeds of galaxies, stars, and planets; the wellspring of seas, rivers, and streams; the life source of forests, fields, and flowers; the eggs from which are hatched alligators and fleas, the promise of life for you and me. Just think: It has taken 14 billion years to shape you and me. If it has taken that length of time- 14 billion years! then surely we are called to hold in reverence and awe the beauty of our own created being. If God has taken all that time to fashion us, then perhaps we are worth something, after all. The marvel is that it all began with fire. And it is to fire that we shall return, into the celestial fire of God's life-giving love, which envelops and enfolds us.

The rhythm and pattern of this book, as I have repeated many times, is circular and spiral, involving a movement of return towards origins. It is a movement which replicates the passage of Jesus back to the Father; it is His eternal rising and ascending transition into which we are drawn. This movement is not simply one towards a previous state of biological existence in infancy, where our relationship to God finds expression in a childlike dependence upon the mothering God, important though such a movement is. Rather, the movement into the mystery of the Divine is a journey in imagination and memory into the origin of all that is, towards the time when we came to birth in the primeval cauldron of fire. I say that the journey is one into memory because, no matter how inchoate, no matter how residual, we bear within our brains memory-traces of our beginnings. If we are able to immerse ourselves in, and identify ourselves with, the wonder of our beginnings, we become increasingly sensitised to our human becoming, which we share with the seas and the stars. It is then, and only then, we become capable of adopting a stance of profound humility and reverence before all that is.

This movement is neither academic nor speculative, for the very future of the human race depends upon an acknowledgement that our lives are intrinsically and intricately bound up with and enmeshed in the whole of created reality. We do not exist in isolation but form an integral part of the whole cosmos, something to which John Donne draws attention in *The Bell*:

> No man is an Island, intire of itselfe; every man is a peece of the Continent, a part of the maine; if a Clod bee washed away by the Sea, Europe is the lesse, as well as if a Promontorie were ... any man's death diminishes me, because I am involved in Mankinde; And therefore never send to know for whom the bell tolls; it tolls for thee.[1]

The degree to which we treat our fellow-travellers on this planet - the forests, the seas, the animals, and the insects, particularly those currently on the verge of extinction, to that same degree we are in fact treating ourselves. If human greed, indifference and insensitivity condemn a single species to extinction, we are, in all probability, pronouncing a death sentence upon ourselves (or at least our children's children).

---

[1] J. Donne, *The Bell*, *Devotions upon Emergent Occasions*, In The Oxford Book of English Prose, chosen and edited by Sir Arthur Quiller-Couch, (Oxford: Clarendon Press, 1973) 171-72.

Such is the fragile delicacy of the ecosystem from which we all draw life and are sustained in being.

What I have just written is, of course, an exaggeration and not strictly accurate because, as we well know species have emerged throughout history and blossomed and subsequently yielded to the whole of evolutionary unfolding, which demands that they have their entrances and exits upon the stage of existence and then eventually perish.

However, species which have become extinct did not do so as a result of their own volition; they did not cease to exist as a consequence of their deliberately self-inflicted wounds. By contrast, humans have a unique capacity to shoot themselves in the foot; we possess a staggering degree of hubris which blinds us to the consequences of our actions, unaware that the planet will continue to survive, albeit initially in a polluted and contaminated state, long after the human race has vanished from the face of the earth. People have a tendency to be preoccupied with their own narrow interests and concerns. Thankfully, however, we also possess a wondrous capacity for kindness and generosity, for empathy and love. Perhaps, under the gaze of God, this will be our salvation.

If we allow ourselves to reflect the gaze of God, it will become a little more evident that our place in the universe, although immensely privileged, is still but a part of the interconnected web of creation, cleansed, made beautiful, enlightened, and enriched by the affectionate gaze of God. His enlightening gaze opens the eyes of the mind, whereby we may see more clearly the heavenly spiral of the swirling planets as that essential pattern of movement into which the divine gaze invites and seduces us. The motion of those heavenly spheres is identical to the movement which shapes the dance of life, that movement which draws us, if we so allow, into the heart of God.

It is by engaging is such a dance that we are able to discern the truth that in our end is our beginning and that in our beginning is our end, and so the dance of life continues. As Jesus ben Sirach reminds us, "In all that you do remember the end of your life, and then you will never sin" (Sir. 7: 16), an insight reinforced and expanded by T S Eliot: "What we call the beginning is often the end/And to make an end is to make a beginning. The end is where we start from."[2]

---

[2]   T.S. Eliot, *Four Quartets*, 47.

Where do we start? Like the whole of creation, we have our beginning in fire. Brian Swimme, in his book *The Universe is a Green Dragon*, invites us to contemplate our origins in the furnace of life:

> We need to start with the story of the universe as a whole. Our emergent cosmos is the fundamental context for all discussions of value, meaning, and purpose, or ultimacy of any sort ...
>
> Imagine that furnace out of which everything came forth. This was a fire that filled the universe, that *was* the universe ... Every point of the cosmos was a point of this explosion of light ... all that we see about us, all that now exists was there at the beginning, in that great burning explosion of light.[3]

We find similar insight at the very beginning of Scripture: God's primal act of creation is a great explosion of light in the act of separating light from darkness (Gen. 1: 3), a creative act emanating from and powered by the gaze of God: "And God saw that it was good." So, too, with subsequent creative acts: the earth and the seas, and God saw that it was good; fruit trees and plants, and God saw that it was good; the sun, moon, and stars, and God saw that it was good; the birds of the air and the fish of the sea, and God saw it was good; woman and

---

[3] B. Swimme, *The Universe is a Green Dragon* (Rochester, Vermont: Bear and Co., 2001) 27.

man, you and me, "And God saw everything that he had made, and, behold, it was very good" (Gen. 1: 26 -31). It is the gaze which calls into being; it is the gaze which gives the light of life; it is the gaze which makes good and beautiful; all that is created. It is for the gaze of God that the psalmist so fervently prayed: "Let thy face shine on thy servant; save me in the steadfast love" (Ps. 31: 16).

The gaze of God is the light of life: the true light that enlightens everyone coming into the world. The gaze of God enkindles the fire of life down through the ages. Life-fire calls to Moses from within the bush: "And the angel of the Lord appeared to him in a flame of fire out of the midst of a bush; and he looked, and lo, the bush was burning, yet it was not consumed" (Ex. 3: 2). Life-fire calls to Moses to bring freedom and new life to the people God has chosen as His own. "And the Lord went before them in a pillar of cloud by day to lead them along the way, and by night in a pillar of fire to give them light that they may travel by day and by night" (Ex. 13: 21). Life-fire leads the people into a land flowing with milk and honey.

Life-fire generates a capacity for remembering. God remembers His covenant on seeing the light captured in the colours of the rainbow. Life-fire is the eternal pledge that the Covenant between God and creation shall never, ever be broken. Hues of violet, indigo, blue, green, yellow, orange, and red delight the eye of God, standing as they do, as the promise that now and through eternity, never again shall the Lord God break his agreement with His people: "This is the sign of the covenant which I make between me and you and *every living creature* that is with you, for all future generations; I set my bow in the cloud, and it shall be a sign of the covenant between me and the earth. When I bring clouds over the earth and the bow is seen in the clouds I will remember my covenant which is between me and you *and every living creature.*" (Gen. 9: 13 - 16, italics added).

God answered the prayer of Elijah with life-fire, which descended to consume the sacrificial offering even though drenched in water, even though the trench surrounding the altar was filled to the brim with water (1 Kings 18: 36). Life-fire became death-fire when it consumed the two captains along with their cohort of fifty men sent by King Ahaziah to

Elijah to summon the prophet into the king's presence (see 2 Kings, 1), a salutary reminder that fire may enlighten our steps, warm us up and cook our food, but it is, at the same time, dangerous and should, like God, be treated with awe, reverence, and respect.

After the years of darkness in exile in Babylon, the children of Israel receive the promise of the life-fire of God: "The sun shall no more be your light by day, nor for brightness shall the moon give light to you by night; but the Lord will be your everlasting light, and your God will be your glory" (Is. 60: 19). That same life-fire erupts in the incarnating of God: "I came to cast [life-fire] on the earth; and would that it were already kindled" (Lk. 14: 49).

Life-fire explodes into newness of a million untold possibilities; life-fire banishes death-darkness at the dawning of everlasting light with the rising of the Son: "Rejoice O earth, in shining splendour, radiant in the brightness of your King! Christ has conquered! Glory fills you! Darkness vanishes forever" (*The Easter Proclamation*). After the dawning of the Eternal Sun, life-fire emboldened the disciples of Jesus as they cowered in a darkened room in Jerusalem. Tongues of fire gave them the new heart fearlessly toproclaim the Good News of freedom. The wonder of it all is that those same tongues of fire will touch our lives, if only we open the door of our hearts to receive the promised light and life. Life-fire is our origin; life-fire is our destiny, as it was the destiny of the two disciples on the road to Emmaus: "Did not our hearts burn [with life-fire] within us while he talked to us on the road, while he opened to us the scriptures?" And they rose that same hour and returned to Jerusalem" (Lk. 24:32-33).

In this final chapter, we shall explore the four activities John of the Cross ascribes to the gaze of God: its cleansing activity; the flowering of all that is beautiful in the heart; the act of enriching and giving meaning to life; and the enlightening of the human mind and the clarifying of human vision. God achieves these four effects much in the same way that He brought everything into being at the beginning of time, through the fondness of His gaze. The cleansing, making beautiful, enriching, and enlightening acts of God are distinct but intertwining functions which operate much in the same way that we ascribe different roles to each Person of the Trinity, who are all equal. Each is eternal, vibrant, creative, loving energy; in constant flux constantly self-generating; constantly self-disclosing; constantly drawing us back to our beginnings, both on the individual and the cosmic level; constantly seducing us; constantly whispering in our ear; constantly inviting us into ever deeper intimacy with Him. All we have to do is to allow God sufficient elbow room in order to achieve His design. However, sometimes we are like a baby, restless and agitated at the mother's breast; other times, like a child who squirms and protests when her mother attempts to wipe her dirty face with a flannel; sometimes like a sullen teenager who sulks when told to be home at a certain time. Perhaps this is why the movement of turning again and again is taking so long. It takes so long because God respects us too much and would never drag us kicking and screaming into union with Him. If freedom is our destiny, then it would be illogical for God to deny us freedom on the journey. As always, the choice is ours.

To return to the main theme of the chapter, let us take a look again at what John writes in the annotation to the 32nd Stanza of the *Spiritual Canticle*:

> it must be known that the look of God works four blessings in the soul namely, that it cleanses, beautifies, enriches and enlightens it, even as he sun, when it sends forth its rays, dries and warms and beautifies and makes resplendent. And after God has set these three blessings in the soul it becomes very pleasing to him because of them and thus he remembers no more ... the sin that it had aforetime.[4]

The four blessings of the gaze of God reflect the rhythm of the changing seasons, and each has a relevance to a particular season of the heart. Without straining the analogy too far, we may interpret the blessing of cleansing as winter blessing; the blessing of beauty as vernal blessing; the blessing of enrichment as summer blessing; and finally, the blessing of enlightenment, the blessing of fruitfulness, as autumn blessing. The blessings of God are always tailored to the need of the present moment, exquisitely sensitive to the change of season within the human heart. Step by step, let's allow the richness

---

[4] John of the Cross, *The Complete Works of St John of the Cross,* Vol. II, Translated and Edited by E Allison Peers, revised edition (Westminster, Maryland: The Newman Press, 1953, 347. (In a later redaction, the phrase "these last three blessings" is corrected to read "these last four blessings").

of what John has written to unfold, beginning with the blessing of cleansing.

The Winter Blessing: Cleansing

Many are the ways in which the gaze of God cleanses us, and for the sake of simplicity, this part of the chapter will concern itself with only three aspects of His cleansing activity: washing, purifying, and healing:

Washing

The washing of baptism will not be addressed in this section because, firstly, it would take us outside the scope of the book and the theme we are attempting to explore. Secondly, baptism has been the subject of much theological reflection from apostolic times, by persons far more capable than I; thirdly, much reflection on baptism tends to be static, regarding baptism as a sacrament, as some *thing* rather than as an ongoing event; hence, theological reflection, in some measure at least, loses the dynamic character of μυστηριον (that mystical truth which the gaze of God brings to birth in the minds and hearts of those who seek Him) and, as such, may well run counter to the dynamics of spiritual development, which is the object of our present enquiry; fourthly, baptism, whether administered to infant or adult, is a one-time event, never to be repeated, whereas the cleansing gaze of God is constantly active in our lives. Finally, the gaze of God is not restricted to those who have been baptised; God's gaze shines on all women, men, and particularly children, irrespective of their faith or lack thereof; God's gaze enlightens all that is, is all inclusive, enveloping all things, and most preciously of all, need not be earned or merited.

In passing, however, we may note that there is an important connection between baptism and the blessings which the gaze of God confers upon the human spirit. This concerns the connection we find between baptism and the fourth blessing bestowed by the gaze of God, namely, the blessing of enlightenment. This link finds expression in the symbol of the lighted candle received at baptism: "Receive the light of Christ and keep true to your baptism by a blameless life." The connection between the washing of baptism and enlightenment may be traced back to the second century when Justin Martyr, in his first Apology, writes, "And this washing is called illumination, because they who learn these things are illuminated in their understandings. And in the name of Jesus Christ, who was crucified under Pontius Pilate, and in the name of the Holy Ghost, who through the prophets foretold all things about Jesus, he who is illuminated is washed" (Chapter 61).[5] And, conversely, the one who is washed is illuminated in the spirit of understanding.

In everyday life, the act of washing bears little relationship to illumination. Much of our experience of washing may be onerous and tedious: washing the dishes (or stacking the dishwasher); doing the laundry; washing the car; cleaning the windows; watering the lawn; to the extent that, if we can afford it, we employ others to do the washing. Washing also inevitably implies the presence of dirt which, in the context of spiritual development, is most unfortunate because there is a tendency to identify dirt with the stain of sin, or at least some sort of moral defect. Consciousness of being "soiled," "stained" and "unwholesome" works against our best interests in two ways. In the first place, it focuses our attention on ourselves and our own shortcomings instead of remaining

---

[5] New Advent, http://www.newadvent.org/fathers/0126.htm, accessed 05/11/2014.

focused on the hand of God, who holds us in being with love and compassion. In chapter 1 I referred to the teacher who reprimanded the naughty schoolboy by pointing to her eyes with two fingers of her right hand and then pointing those same fingers towards the front of the hall. I used the example to show how, if we wish to progress along the spiritual path, we must have our eyes fixed on the face of God and not allow ourselves to be distracted or discouraged by our own failings (real or imagined).

The second way in which focus on our own shortcomings and unworthiness impedes our entering more deeply into the mystery of the Divine is that it may make us reluctant to face God in prayer, much in the same way that Adam and Eve hid in the garden at the sound of His voice. If we feel unworthy, tarnished in some way, failing to live up to ideals (imposed either from without or within); if we come into the presence of God with thoughts of our unworthiness, then it becomes difficult, if not impossible, to relax or feel at ease. At times such as these, perhaps we have no need to be unduly concerned because the Lord Jesus brings us assurance and comfort through the word of Scripture: "You are already made clean by the word that I have spoken to you. Abide in me and I in you" (Jn. 15:3-4a). For the evangelist, it is the Word made flesh which has already cleansed the spirit; for his namesake, John of the Cross, it is the gaze of the Father which makes us clean and whole. And the beauty of it is that it has already happened, it continues to happen, and it will do so into eternity.

Does such an approach lead to complacency? We don't need to bother because God will take care of everything? We can do anything we like because God will forgive us? Yet if we have our eyes fixed on the God who loves us, we respond by reflecting that love, wishing always to serve and love with profound gratitude and humility. Of course, we shall make mistakes; of course, we shall act from motives which are less than honourable; of course, we shall succumb to self-pity or envy or resentment. They are merely clouds which, for a brief time, obscure the rays of the sun but do not affect the essential nature of our being beloved children of God.

Because of the negative connotation associated with cleansing - at least in the spiritual domain, where it refers to a cleansing from the stain of sin - we may readily embrace the notion that, in the sight of God and in our own estimation, we are not worth much at all and stand in constant need of cleansing and purification. This negative connotation has been reinforced by the teaching we received as children, augmented by a whole tradition which has bolstered such self-appraisal, reinforced by liturgical and sacramental practices. With it, comes a tendency to take ourselves far too seriously. As a result, when it comes to our experience of washing, we have lost so much of the fun that can be had with washing and splashing. Watch children in a paddling pool scream with delight as they frolic in the water. There is the hand of God.

When I reflect on the gaze of God in its cleansing work, I am often drawn back to one of my earliest memories, that of being bathed by my mother, something which was sometimes a less than-relaxing experience due to her exuberance and sense of fun. The image which stands out in my mind is one of sitting in an old white tin bath with a dark blue rim, in front of a roaring coal fire in winter, receiving the winter blessing from God. My mother's arm encircled my body as she washed me, and as she bathed me, she would sing to me. Unfortunately, one of the songs popular during the early 1940s was Dinah Shore's version of *"Yes, My Darling Daughter."*

My mother would lift me high out of the water and plunge me back in time with the rhythm of the music, singing at the top of her voice while I screamed with delight. At one time, a visiting aunt protested that I was a boy, not a girl. To which my mother replied, "Yes, but I love that song!" Thus it was that bathing became associated in memory with fun, music, and laughter, and a blurring of gender identity. How fortunate, how blessed to be bathed in the waters of God's abiding love. How even more fortunate to become aware of being smiled on with affection by the God of infinite tenderness. That is the cleansing of which John speaks.

Like the rainbow, the cleansing winter gaze of God admits of a variety of different hues and expressions, possessing two faces: one snug and warm, the other, barren and dark. As noted above, the cleansing work of God can be light-hearted and playful as was my early experiences of being bathed by my mother. Into this same category falls the image of a woman who returns from a night out with dear friends and sits at her dressing table, ruminating on the pleasure of the evening, softly wiping the makeup from her face as she prepares for bed. This gentle, tender cleansing is one we find in the cooling balm of ointment which relieves the pain of stings and cuts, a cleansing which serves as an act of compassion and healing. Such, at times, is the gentle, soft, almost imperceptibly mellowing activity of divine cleansing.

But it's not always like that. At other times, the cleansing of God can feel extremely abrasive and harsh, such as when we are faced with the demand to be cleansed of all that impedes us from closer union with God: cleansed from the wilfulness of clinging to our resentments; cleansed from an inflated sense of self-importance; cleansed from our inability to tolerate the frailties of others and the shame of our own weakness; cleansed from our dogmatism and self-reliance; cleansed from our attachments to all that offers a spurious assurance of safety and comfort; cleansed from adopting a superior attitude towards those less fortunate; cleansed from needing to be thought well of, to be noticed and to be appreciated; cleansed from reacting to the hurt of being taken for granted.

Did I miss anything? What about lust? What about harbouring thoughts of a sexual nature? I may be wrong, but I believe sexual desire to be an inherent feature of what it means to be human. Fourteen billion years have gone into the fashioning of our sexuality, so apart from the cold and joyless duty of propagation of the species, there must be some room for playfulness and fun. The whole point of priestly celibacy and the vow of chastity taken by religious is that it entails giving up something very precious, something very pleasurable, admittedly having more weight but with the same fundamental intent underlying the practice of giving up sweets for Lent. With the obvious exception of using another person solely for one's own sexual gratification and, more worthy of condemnation, the inhumanity of abuse in all its forms, our sexual nature does not impede us from entering more closely into union with God. If sexual desire were to act as an impediment to entry into the kingdom of God, why on earth does Jesus consort with prostitutes, find obvious pleasure in their company, and put them at the head of the line when it comes to entering the kingdom of His Father? It is such a shame that of the Ten Commandments, only two get pride of place, each concerning disordered sexual activity. Perhaps, just perhaps, the call to freedom, not licence, includes the call to be free from sexual hang-ups.

Purifying

The need for cleansing of all that inhibits freedom requires the gaze of God to purify the human spirit, which brings us to a consideration of the second aspect of God's cleansing activity: the purifying activity of His loving gaze. From fire we are made; from fire we are fashioned. It stands to reason, therefore, that as fire is the means of our origin, so fire is the means by which we attain our destiny, enfolded and united in the bosom of the Father. Eliot finishes his *Four Quartets* with a quotation from Julian of Norwich: "And all shall be well and/All manner of thing shall be well." The time when all shall be well is that time "when the tongues of flame are in-folded,/Into the crowned knot of fire/And the fire and the rose are one."[6] That is when, in the fullness of time, at the *pleroma*, all manner of thing shall be well. Our destiny resides in our being in-folded in all-that-is and in all-that-is being in-folded into us. But first, we have to undergo a process of purification to remove the scales from our eyes so we may see more clearly that to which the gaze of God impels us. And this is accomplished through the purifying activity of fire.

---

[6] T.S. Eliot, "Little Gidding," *Four Quartets* (London: Faber & Faber, 1979) 48.

This act of purifying is a winter experience because it is only during winter that we have need of fire to warm us; during summer, we give no thought to turning on the central heating. It is a winter moment at the core of which lies the Greek word for fire, πυρ (pur), as I mentioned in chapter 2. Such was the intensity of the longing for God felt by John of the Cross that he implored his God: "O Living Flame of love/ That tenderly wounds my soul in its deepest centre - perfect me now."[7] For John, the Flame of God is the Flame of Love, a flame which cleanses and purifies, a flame which makes holy.

Throughout history there has been a certain tendency in religious circles to associate the need for purification with an emphasis on our sinfulness and unworthiness before God. This, in turn, has led to some rather disastrous consequences in some instances, such as self-flagellation and anorexia. Rather than interpreting purification as a sort of window-cleaning activity or an act of cleaning our glasses so we may see better, we have invested it with graphic images of the fire of purgatory and the flames of hell.

---

[7] John of the Cross, *Living Flame of Love, The Complete Works of St. John of the Cross,* vol. III, Translated and Edited by E Allison Peers, revised edition. (The Newman Press, 1953) 17.

A preoccupation with sinfulness and unworthiness extends to the celebration of Eucharist, as I mentioned in chapter 3. When we are invited to share at the table of the Lord, we are called upon first to acknowledge our sinfulness, not once but three times, and resort to superlatives to describe the nature of our failings: "through my fault, through my fault, through my most grievous fault; Lord, be merciful to me, a sinner; Lord, I am not worthy that you should enter under my roof." While acknowledging that we are not perfect, a focus upon sin engenders a negative view of self, and when so many people suffer from a poor self-image in the first place then this only makes matters worse. Much of my work as a therapist involves helping people to change the way they view themselves by replacing the negative with the positive, helping them to free themselves from the tyranny of the "should." In my therapeutic work, when faced with someone who uses the word *"should"*, I invariably suggest, as gently as I can, that the word "should" be replaced with the word "could" because that simple change introduces a note of freedom and lessens the burden of an expectation imposed from without: "I should phone my mother-in-law" is an imperative which brooks no exception;

"I could phone my mother-in-law" means that a sense of obligation is lifted, and I am free to act as I wish.

Without gainsaying the pain involved in many an act by which God cleanses and purifies the heart, we find a beautiful image of this whole process in the prophesy of Malachi (Mal. (3:2-4):

> For he is like a refiner's fire and the fuller's soap; he will sit as a refiner and purifier of silver, and he will purify the sons of Levi and refine them like gold and silver, till they present right offerings to the Lord.

The image is that of a silversmith who acts with supreme patience, hovering over the crucible, applying the bellows to increase the heat. As the metal gradually becomes molten, the impurities contained therein bubble to the surface. The silversmith draws a paddle across the surface to remove the impurities and then repeats the process. After many, many applications of bellows and paddle, nearly all impurities are removed from the silver, and then, and then only, the silversmith gazes into the surface of the metal, where he sees clearly reflected the image of his own countenance. And so it is with God. In the act of purifying, little by little, God cleanses the human spirit until eventually, He can gaze into the soul and see reflected there the image of His own Divine face.

Sometimes people complain that adversity and misfortune come into their lives because they have sinned. They believe that they deserve to suffer because of some real or imagined offence. Adversity and misfortune are not the work of God. Nothing could be further from the truth. It's not as though God is punitive, taking us to task for all our failures and inadequacies; it's rather the events of daily life purge the spirit of the detritus which accumulates as sediment at the bottom of the soul, adding weight to the spirit which slows down the journey into the mystery of God. The soul needs the divine silversmith to draw the paddle of his compassion across the surface of our being and relieve us of all that sullies the spirit. The scouring of the human spirit is often painful, yet perhaps we can draw consolation from the fact that as well as being the Divine Silversmith, God is also the Divine Physician healing our wounds.

Healing

In the epilogue to his book *The Restoration of the Self,* Heinz Kohut writes

Nowhere in art have I encountered a more accurately painted description of man's yearning to achieve the restoration of his self than that contained in three terse sentences in O'Neill's play *The Great God Brown* ... "Man is born broken. He lives by mending. The grace of God is the glue." Could the essence of the pathology of modern man's self be stated more impressively?[8]

If I may be permitted to paraphrase Eugene O'Neill's words by adding the thought that perhaps, after John of the Cross, it is perhaps the gaze of God rather than grace which brings about healing in the human heart. As Teresa writes, "And God is always there if you feel wounded. He kneels over the earth like a divine physician and His love thaws the holy in us."[9] The thaw which occurs in response to the warmth of God's healing gaze is a gradual process. As I mentioned in chapter 1, citing George Vaillant's book *Adaptation to Life,* one of the major advances in surgical technique in the nineteenth century was for the surgeon not to interfere with the healing process but to give the wound time to heal. And so it is with the healing gaze of God. It takes time.

---

[8] H. Kohut, *The Restoration of the Self,* (International Universities Press, 1977) 287.

[9] St Teresa of Avila, *When the Holy Thaws*, in D. Landinsky, *Love Poems from God* (Penguin Putnam Group, 2002) 291.

But nothing is simple or straightforward. There's usually a snag. The snag in this instance lies in our unwillingness to allow God to get close enough to heal our wounds. We are like a child who gets a splinter in his finger and goes running to his mother. The moment the mother goes to her workbox and takes out a needle, the child, fearing that the pain of the needle would be far worse than the pain of the splinter, immediately stuffs his hand under his armpit and requires a certain amount of coaxing before he will allow his mother to remove the splinter.

The three winter blessings, of cleansing, purifying, and healing, lay the soul open to receive the blessing of spring, that rich gaze of God which makes us beautiful. As we move from winter to spring, we carry with us the awareness that, like the seasons of the year, the seasons of the spirit fold back on themselves and are repeated, time and time again. We are never finished with the need to be cleansed; we constantly stand in need of being purified; and the wounds of time demand that the gaze of God bring comfort and healing.

The Spring Blessing: Making Beautiful

If we take a brief excursus into the realm of metaphysics (it will be very brief, I promise you), we learn that beauty finds itself in the company of the good and the true as a transcendental property of being. Scholastic philosophers claim that all that exists (being) possesses certain properties and that each of these properties enjoys a unity of being with other properties by the very fact that they exist. Hence, it is that where the gaze of God makes beautiful, it also makes good; where the gaze of God makes good, it also makes true. Once more, we come across the profound insight of the sacred author, where the gaze of God creates and the power of His gaze makes good. It is a creative act, continuous and repetitive, which leads the human spirit towards perfection, a trajectory favoured by those writers on spiritual growth who place perfection as the goal of the spiritual journey. By contrast, I would suggest that the goal of the spiritual journey is not perfection but freedom. The reason for this lies in the structure and essence of human nature: Perfection demands wholeness and completion, and human beings are, by nature, incomplete, and forever open to the possibility of growth, reflecting the nature of the cosmos, which is in a permanent state of expansion. Perfection means there is no possibility of further growth, yet we shall forever be open to growth even into eternity.

Let us return to the topic in hand. God reveals His holy face in the newness and beauty of the springtime of the soul, a time of bringing forth new life with the radiant colours of daffodil, bluebell, and crocus, of cherry and apple blossom; a time of joy-filled activity of lambs gambolling in the meadows; a time of promise and new beginnings; a time to celebrate the beauty of nature, the beauty of all that is, an Easter time of rising to new life."And God saw that it was very good" (Gen. 1:31). It is a time of special blessing, of a call to deeper intimacy with God: In the introduction I wrote that our spiritual identity is formed in a way which reflects the manner in which our emotional, psychological, and social identity is formed, namely, we become that by which we are addressed by others, primarily our mothers. Our spiritual identity is formed by the multiple ways we reflect the gaze of God. And the manner in which we reflect the beauty of God's gaze is by becoming beautiful, not only in the sight of the Lord but also in our own eyes. We become beautiful because we are loved, not for what we do but for who we are and who we shall become. Our becoming beautiful is the flowering of a love affair with God, a love affair which finds one of its more enduring and poetic expressions in the Song of Songs, a series of songs which down through the ages have described the love affair of God and creation: "My Beloved speaks and says to me: Arise, my love, my fair one, and come away; for lo, the winter is past, the rain is over and gone. The flowers appear on the earth, the time of singing has come, and the voice of the turtledove is heard in our land" (S.of S. 2:10-12).

For Kahlil Gibran, beauty is life:

> Beauty is life when life unveils her holy face.
> But you are life and you are the veil.
> Beauty is eternity gazing at itself in a mirror.
> But you are eternity and you are the mirror.[10]

Beauty lies in the forgiving of God. The child who is disconsolate because she has quarrelled with her best friend is tucked up in bed by her mother, who tells her not to mind because tomorrow will be another day, and she will be able

---

[10] K. Gibran, *The Prophet*, (Originally published in 1923 by Alfred A. Knopf, Kindle edition, Chapter 9, loc. 601).

to make up with her friend. Hence the assurance of a fresh start with all the troubles of yesterday forgotten, swallowed up in the bright promise of dawn. Beauty is the new beginning, the fresh start which comes with reconciliation. It sounds so incredibly easy that there must be a catch.

And a catch there surely is, namely, it lies in having the courage to take God at His word. As Pádraic Pearse writes in his poem *The Fool:*

> For this I have heard in my heart, that a man shall scatter, not hoard,
> Shall do the deed of to-day, nor take thought of tomorrow's teen,
> Shall not bargain or huxter with God; or was it a jest of Christ's
> And is this my sin before men, to have taken Him at His word?[11]

All we have to do is to take God at His word; basically, taking God at His word is what we call a profession of faith. "Do you believe that I love you?" "Yes, Lord, I believe." That's really all it takes.

The Summer Blessing: Enrichment

There are three principal ways in which the gaze of God enriches the human spirit: We are enriched, paradoxically,

---

[11] P.H. Pearse, *The Fool* (Electronic edition compiled by Pádraig Bambury, CELT: Corpus of Electronic Texts: a project of University College, Cork, www.ucc.ie/celt, 1998, 2010).

by becoming poor before God, where poverty is understood as complete reliance upon God rather than upon our own resources and efforts; we are enriched by having our spirit enlarged and expanded under the gaze of God, leading to a broader vision of what the Lord is achieving in and through us and a deeper sensitivity towards the working of the Spirit; and we are enriched through a generosity of heart which prompts a gifting of self, an outreach to share with others our time, energy, and material resources.

A. Richness through Poverty

The gaze of God makes us rich in the same manner that He endows the human spirit with the three other blessings of cleansing, making beautiful, and enlighten-ment. God confronts us with the paradox that we become rich to the degree to which we empty ourselves and stand in poverty before His face. In his second letter to the Corinthians, Paul appeals for funds for the church in Jerusalem (see also 1 Cor. 16:1-5). He reminds the Corinthians that they become rich through the poverty of Christ Jesus: "For you know the grace of our Lord Jesus Christ, that though he was rich, yet for your sake he became poor, so that by his poverty you might become rich" (2 Cor. 8:9). Paul is keen to emphasise that we are all one in the body of Christ and that we come to the Father by emulating the pattern of the life and death of Jesus. In other words, we become rich through a process of self-emptying. This self-emptying involves a letting go of our prejudices; our self-destructive negative thoughts about our own value before God; our impatience with ourselves and others; our regrets over failures of the past; our resentments and critical attitudes; in fact, all that impedes our growth into freedom. Poverty implies, essentially, that we travel with light steps into the kingdom of our God. As Jesus recommends, "Carry no purse, no bag, no sandals" (Lk. 10: 4). Spiritual poverty does not mean a state of economic or social distress but rather expresses an attitude of dependence. Poverty, in this sense, describes a relationship in which one is aware of being powerless before God. As John of the Cross expresses it, *Todo y Nada* (God is everything and we are nothing). Poverty implies a journey into emptiness, a journey into the nothingness of The Cloud of Unknowing.

Experience of being powerless leads to entering more completely into the process of conversion, into reliance upon God rather than upon our own natural resources. According to Bill Meissner, the Jesuit scholar, the experience of powerlessness, paradoxically yet again, has power to change our lives:" Among the experiences which are personally transformative is that of powerlessness, particularly the kind of powerlessness that arises when one steps out of the world one knows best. Because it loosens a person from familiar sources of cultural and social identity, from personal and social forms of security, powerlessness is both painful and disorienting. It throws us back on our interior resources. If these too have been diminished, then one is forced into that open space where the creature stands finally before God: a situation which essentially defines human being but which is easily concealed beneath the socially constructed and secure fabric of the human world."[12]

A second defining feature of poverty is the need to wait. Consciousness of being powerless engenders an attitude of total

---

[12] W.W. Meissner, *Primacy of Spiritual Experience in Theological Reflection,* (Boston: Lonergan Workshop Journal, vol. IV) 106.

dependence upon the Other, of expectant waiting for the One who comes. A stance of patient waiting before God engenders a longing and yearning in the heart which nothing other than the touch of God can assuage. This longing is beautifully expressed by the psalmist: "I wait for the Lord, my soul waits, and in his word I hope; my soul waits for the Lord more than watchmen for the morning, more than watchmen for the morning" (Ps. 130:5-6). We find the same theme in Psalm 40: "I waited patiently for the Lord; he inclined to me and heard my cry. He drew me up from the desolate pit." (Ps. 40:1-2).

The prophet who expresses the call to wait patiently most clearly is Habakkuk. It is probable that Habakkuk came on the scene in the decade leading up to the Babylonian invasion of Israel in 597 BCE.[13] The crisis facing Habakkuk was more one of faith than of political or military disaster, although it must be said that the crisis of faith had its roots in the military threat facing Israel. The very foundations of the Israelite belief system were being undermined. Habakkuk wrestled with the perceived contradiction between the promises of God and

---

[13] For the historical background, see J. Bright, *A History of Israel*, (London and Beccles: S C M Press, 1970).

the experience of having been abandoned by Him. This crisis of faith became even more pressing in the light of what lay ahead (Hab. 1:5-11) How is it that God, who sees so much evil perpetrated against His chosen ones, does not intervene? The only option for Habakkuk was to face, as did Abraham, the long delay between promise and fulfilment. The delay accounts for the fact that the word is to be written down and not come immediately to fulfilment, that there will be a delay of indeterminate length between promise and fulfilment. Not only that, the inference drawn by the prophet is that the interval between promise and completion is the very ground of divine activity. No matter what happens, no matter the trials which Israel has to endure, the conviction remains that Yahweh is God alone and has the power to deliver His people (Hab. 1:12). All they have to do is to wait patiently for the unfolding of the divine purpose based on the conviction that "the vision awaits its time; it hastens to the end - it will not lie. If it seems slow, wait for it, it will surely come, it will not delay ... the righteous shall live by faith" (Hab. 2:2-4).

Such were the sentiments which marked the lives of so many of the faithful women of the OT. The scriptures constantly return to the theme of emptiness, more specifically in terms of physical emptiness portrayed by the barren women of scripture: Sarah (Gen. 16:1); Rebekah (Gen. 25:21); Rachel (Gen. 30:1-2); the mother of Samson (Jg. 13:3); Hannah (1Sam. 1-2); and, in the New Testament, Elizabeth (Lk. 1:7), thus demonstrating that the gift of life resides in the hands of God, the God who turns poverty into riches, the God who makes use of the weak and powerless to confound the strong.

Because these women were human, they were not perhaps as faithful as they might have been, women capable of resentment and bitterness, deviousness and guile, callousness and spite. However, for all their human frailty, they represent the *anawim,* or the Poor Ones who look to the Lord for rescue: Because Sarah was childless, she dealt harshly with Hagar, her maid, who had Abraham's child when Sarah had longed for a child of her own (Gen. 16:6). Sarah laughed in disbelief, just as Abraham had before her (Gen. 17:17), at the prospect of conceiving a child at the age of ninety. Rebekah, wife of Isaac (קֵחָ, "he will laugh"), was barren and conceived only when Isaac interceded with the Lord. Imagine her chagrin at being dependent on the prayer of her husband, as if her own prayers weren't good enough, and God only listened to men. Rachel envied her sister, Leah (Gen. 30:1), who was fertile while she herself was barren. Then, as Scripture says, "God remembered Rachel" (Gen. 30: 22), but only after years of (not so) patient waiting. The angel of the Lord appeared to the mother of Samson and said, "Behold, you are barren and have no children; but you shall conceive and bear a son" (Jg. 13:3). Hannah prayed to the Lord out of the depths of her distress, and whose prayer was eventually answered (1 Sam. 1:13ff).

In the New Testament, too, we find Elizabeth, who was childless and advanced in years yet, in God's good time, she conceived and gave birth to John. For God, a day is as a thousand years, and a thousand years are as a day. The in-breaking of God occurs according to His mind, and all we can do is wait, taking little consolation from the words of Longfellow: "Though the mills of God grind slowly/Yet they grind exceeding small;/Though with patience he stands waiting,/With exactness grinds he all."[14]

---

[14] H. Rawson and M. Milner,(ed.) *The Oxford Dictionary of American Quotations,* (Oxford: University Press, 2006) 289.

Waiting is the condition of the Poor Ones who place their confidence in the God Who saves, a confidence born of hope and rooted in trust. "Because the poor are despoiled, because the needy groan, I will now arise, says the Lord; I will place him in the safety for which he longs" (Ps. 12:5).The rich do not have to go on a waiting list in order to have an operation. Not so for the poor. However, the poor in spirit are those who are blessed by God. The Poor Ones acknowledge their position of inferiority before God, as did the publican in the temple (Lk. 18: 9ff). The Poor Ones are the listeners, those who hear the Word addressed to their hearts, those who attend in both senses of the word: attend in the sense of being present, and attend in sense of paying attention. Poverty implies a listening stance before God, waiting for an answer, unlike Pilate in Bacon's essay on truth: "What is truth? said jesting Pilate, and would not stay for an answer."[15] The poor are the patient ones who wait, possibly for a lifetime, for an answer. Our relationship with God blossoms to the extent that we are patient and wait.

---

[15] F. Bacon, *Essays, Civil and Moral. Vol. III, Part 1. The Harvard Classics*, (New York: F. Collier & Son,. www.bartleby.com/3/1/. accessed 11/04/2014).

"The kingdom of God is as if a man should scatter seed upon the ground, and should sleep and rise night and day, and the seed should sprout and grow, he knows not how" (Mk. 4: 26- 27). It's no use to dig up the seed to see if it has germinated; neither is it any use to force-feed the seed to make it grow all the more quickly. It just doesn't work. We have to wait in patient hope that the earth will produce "first the blade, then the ear, then the full grain in the ear" (Mk. 4:28). So often in our journey into the mystery of the Divine, we stand in the way, and then we have the temerity to blame God for our lack of progress or interpret our confusion and darkness as God's gift of desolation, given to test us or purify us in some way, when it is nothing of the sort. If we stand in the way, if we rely on our own meagre resources rather than place ourselves in the divine presence and wait in patience of spirit, then we are inviting failure. Hope lies in the waiting, not taking matters into our own hands. Sometimes, people in the early stages of spiritual development become overly concerned about progress, as if by their own striving they can proceed more rapidly along the path, and they become impatient, or despondent, with their apparent lack of movement and are not too enamoured with the prospect of letting things unfold according to the rhythm of God.

B. Richness through Increased Sensitivity

Someone I accompanied on her journey into the mystery of the Divine wrote in an email, "One thing which has emerged during my daily prayer experience and continued attempt at working through the spiritual exercises has been to see things with new eyes. I have developed a greater appreciation of the little things in life - that sense of gratefulness and hope."[16] Insight comes from revelation and being open to the prompting of the Spirit. In Revelation 21:5 we read, "And he who sat upon the throne said, 'Behold I make all things new." Becoming increasingly open to the possibility of gaining new insight is a blessing conferred by the gaze of God. We are enriched by the expanding of the soul and a widening breadth of vision. The movement is away from the particular, the concrete, the specific, towards an embrace of the universal; it is a movement away from the actual, which may tempt us to throw up our hands in despair, towards immersing ourselves in the promise

---

[16] M. Dawe, Personal communication by email.

of the possible. It is the journey from the darkness of Good Friday to the glorious dawn of Easter Day. The gaze of God which enriches the spirit may cause great pain because the spirit which grows, matures, and expands becomes increasingly aware of its own poverty. This, in turn, engenders an ache and longing to be one with God; we chafe at the restraints which the human condition imposes upon us, yet, even so, because nothing is lost in the providence of God, such suffering brings with it a healing of the earth.

Sensitivity is an openness to the touch of God, an awareness of abiding presence; it is also acceptance of the suffering such sensitivity brings: awareness of our oneness with all who suffer in war; all who grieve the death of children; all who are deprived of liberty; all who lack food and clean water and a roof over their heads. The sensitivity born of the gaze of God allows us to acknowledge our unity with the mother who blushes with embarrassment because she has to resort to a food bank in order to feed her family. Yet as valuable our awareness is of our being one with the whole family of humanity, it does not rest there. Because of our common origin with the whole of created reality, our enrichment by the tender gaze of God increases our sensitivity towards the planet, making us conscious of how limited are the natural resources of our world; putting a brake on our natural acquisitiveness and greed; preventing our disfiguring the face of the earth by dropping litter; having care not to waste food. All these measures are sacraments, displaying that concern and reverence which reflect the gaze of God. Sometimes, it is easy to consign all things spiritual to the realm of the impractical as if the soul is concerned exclusively with matters having no practical relevance.

Sensitivity to our oneness with all created reality allows us to make sense of the way in which God responds to our prayer. Sometimes, we gain the impression that God is not listening to our prayer, and if He does, then He doesn't respond in the way we would wish. How is it, we may ask, that Jesus responds immediately to the pleas of the leper, the centurion, the widow of Nain, Martha, and Mary, yet the Father appears to turn a deaf ear to our reasonable requests for healing? What is that all about? I venture to suggest that if we are sufficiently sensitised to our being at one with all created reality, then we can acknowledge that, in prayer, we become channels of

God's abiding care for all that is, and that in us and through us, the power of God operates to bring blessing, healing, and comfort to those most in need. No prayer goes unanswered; no plea goes unattended. It's just that the infinity of God's love finds expression in response to our prayer by touching the lives of countless others, bringing them comfort and healing. Being limitless, God's response is such that it transcends our limited field of vision, and if we experience disappointment or frustration at God's apparent lack of response, then perhaps we need to have a little more sensitivity to the way He always responds to the prayer of His children. Furthermore, when our prayer becomes urgent, then our focus is upon our own needs rather than upon the will of the Father; prayer then becomes directed towards self rather than directed towards God and thereby ceases to be prayer.

C. Richness through Self-Gift

There is an old saying that it is more blessed to give than to receive, and the richness conferred by the gaze of God amply rewards generosity of spirit, for as Scripture says, God loves a cheerful giver. We are liberated, set free, by the self-gift of the Son of God, and under the gaze of God, we are invited to share liberally all that we have received and that calls for self-sacrifice. In his book *Markings,* Dag Hammerskjold, the Swedish diplomat who served as the second secretary-general of the United Nations until his death in a plane crash in September 1961, reflects on the nature of sacrifice:

> The price you must pay for your own liberation through another's sacrifice is that you in turn must be willing to liberate in the same way irrespective of the consequence to yourself.[17]

Also, Alan Jones writes:

> There is no way that the Christian can escape the call to sacrifice. It is central to his or her interpretation of reality. Indeed human creativity and the hope for fulfilment presuppose it. The creation of the simplest thing requires sacrifice because, in order to create, something has to be given up: time, energy and alternative possibilities.[18]

Self gift doesn't have to be dramatic, but it has to be a constant feature of spiritual development. And it certainly doesn't demand a martyr complex. Self-gift stems from a sensitivity to the needs of others and also, at times, a sensitivity to one's own personal needs. This reminds me of

---

[17] D. Hammerskjold, *Markings,* Translated from the Swedish by Leif Sjöberg, (London: W. H. Auden, 1966) 163.

[18] A. Jones, *Exploring Spiritual Direction,* (Seabury Press, 1999) 113.

an incident many years ago when I drove home to visit my parents. In my hometown, there was a care home run by a religious order of sisters. In this care home lived a priest who was a member of my congregation, and it came into my mind to pay him a visit, as I was going to pass the gate of the care home where he lived. I remembered him as being a rather irascible and cantankerous individual, and I didn't much like him. And I felt that he probably wouldn't appreciate a visit. Not only that, I decided that it was a little inconvenient, as it was nearly lunchtime, and my mother was preparing a meal, so I decided not to bother. As I drove past the front gates of the home, a vivid picture imprinted itself on my mind: I was at the gates of heaven at the moment of my death, and there stood Jesus to welcome me, and His first words to me were, "You so-and-so! You could at least have made an effort to visit the sick. That surely wasn't too much to ask." So with this image in mind, I turned the car around and went to visit the old man. I presented myself at the reception desk, gave my name, and asked to see the priest. Eventually, he came shuffling down the corridor in the care of a nurse. He didn't seem a bit pleased to see me, and when the nurse suggested that he take me into the visitors' room for a chat, he turned to her, without giving me so much as a glance, and said, "It's lunchtime, and I want my dinner." The nurse reassured him that his lunch would be kept warm, but he insisted that he wanted his lunch there and then. So after a brief good-bye, I took my leave.

As I passed through the gates of the care home, I cocked my eye to heaven and said, "See, I told you that it wouldn't be worthwhile" only to receive the reply, "Oh, but it was worthwhile. You have no idea." And then He showed me in my imagination all the people throughout the world who had been touched, healed, and comforted by my gesture. The smallest sacrifice we make has a worth of infinite value.

The Autumn Blessing: Enlightenment

Within the New Testament, there are frequent allusions to the way we come to understand the presence and activity of God in our lives as a process of enlightenment. Jesus proclaims himself as "the light of the world" (Jn. 8:12), anyone who walks in Him will have the light of life, enjoying a vision by which one more clearly sees the way in which the Spirit is at work in the soul. Paul, in the second chapter of his letter to the Philippians, encourages his readers to have within them the mind of Christ, to see things differently, to see that triumph comes through failure and exaltation comes through self-emptying. What to us is up, for God may well be down, what to us is down is up; what is lost is found; what is poor is rich; what is death is life. What a topsy-turvy world we create when we allow God to enter and take possession of our lives. Another view of enlightenment may be seen in the hymn *"Come Holy Ghost"* which paints a picture of the Holy Spirit as the finger of God's right hand, reminiscent of Michelangelo's painting of creation on the roof of the Sistine Chapel where the finger of God reaches out to give life to Adam. The hymn also portrays the Spirit as the promise of God "teaching little ones to speak and understand." For it is from the mouths of children in the Temple that the praise of God issues forth: "But when the chief priests and the scribes saw the wonderful things that he did and the children crying out in the temple … they were indignant, and they said to him, 'Do you hear what they are saying?' And Jesus said to them, 'Yes, have you never read, "Out of the mouths of babes and sucklings thou has brought perfect praise"? (Mt. 21: 15-16). Sometimes, it takes the innocence of a child to perceive and speak the truth, and, by virtue of the fact that the spiritual path is circular, we, in Eliot's words, return to the place where we started and can access that innocence in the depths of our own being.

Again, as we journey into the mystery of the Divine, we are confronted by yet another paradox, for the promise to teach little ones to speak and understand runs counter to conventional wisdom, which dictates that understanding is the prerogative of age, not childhood. Received wisdom has it that advanced years are meant to bring with them a depth of understanding belonging more to the autumn rather than to the spring of life, to that "season of mists and mellow fruitfulness,/Close bosom-friend of the maturing sun."[19] If, as I have repeated time and time again, spiritual development is a spiral movement, then, while remaining faithful to the pattern established by a daily routine of prayer, we recapture some of the trust and innocence of childhood and, in our maturity, we take it a stage further and act upon the understanding we have gained.

---

[19] J. Keats, "Ode to Autumn," in *The Oxford Book of English Verse, 125 - 1918*, Chosen and Edited by Sir Arthur Quiller Couch, Second Edition, (Oxford University Press, 1987) 749.

Immanuel Kant, the philosopher of the Enlightenment, holds that the process of enlightenment is a movement away from a slavish dependence on someone else for guidance towards claiming one's own authority. A lack of confidence in self and reliance upon some external source usually stems from a doubt in our own insight and understanding. If our eyes remain on the God who gazes upon us with such love, we then allow the Spirit to enlighten the eyes of the mind and begin to live by the motto which lies at the heart of the Enlightenment: *Sapere aude!* (Dare to know!). In other words, have courage, like Pádraic H. Pearse, to take God at His word. From Kant's perspective of enlightenment as movement away from dependence upon external authority towards a reliance upon our own, we may interpret the revolutionary movement from the old dispensation enshrined in the *Torah* (the Law of Moses), a dispensation which is reliant upon external authority engraved on tablets of stone, towards an internalisation and personalisation of our response to the call of God enshrined in the New Testament. As Paul writes, "You are a letter from Christ ... written not with ink but with the Spirit of the living God, not on tablets of stone but on tablets of human hearts" (2 Cor. 3: 3).

If we abdicate our responsibility to think for ourselves, we halt the process of spiritual growth. In chapter 3 I noted that the temptation to embrace the certainty promised by an unquestioning conformity to external norms is truly seductive, yet by doing so, we abandon any prospect of achieving personal freedom, freedom which allows us to conform to legitimate authority, both religious and secular, from a position of autonomy, an autonomy which stems from an internal locus of control, not something imposed by external authority. If we exclusively look to external authority to shape our thinking and actions, we violate the principle of what it means truly to be human, truly to be a child of God. Not only that, we also go astray. History is littered with the havoc wreaked by slavish adherence to some warped ideal or to the ranting of some delusional maniac, witness the slaughter and subjugation of the native tribes of South America in the sixteenth century in the name of religion; witness the unbelievable slaughter of the *Shoah* when more than six million people were massacred in the name of racial purity; witness the ethnic cleansing in Bosnia where, in Srebrenica in 1995, more than 8,000 Muslim men and boys were killed and more than twenty-five-thousand people were displaced from their homes; witness the atrocities committed in the name of religion by Islamic State. All these acts of savagery are products of an unquestioning acceptance of orders and, by definition, are inhuman because they result from an abdication of personal responsibility.

Much of the distress I have experienced in my life occurred when I tried to be a strong advocate of personal self-determination, only to have such advocacy interpreted as disloyalty, even heresy, and to have people I liked and admired react with hostility but sometimes with venom. Central to my own belief system lies the conviction that the Son of God became human in order to show us how to be free. Surely the Good News does not demand slavery. Earlier in the book, I reflected that a focus on sin is a negative focus on self, literally a turning away from God. In this case, abrogation of our personal responsibility and our personal dignity by looking to another to impose thoughts and behaviour, when we are perfectly capable of doing so for ourselves, is a turning sideways and a movement away from God.

The seemingly contradictory demands of respect for legitimate authority and the call to be fully human and fully alive through a process of self-determination face us with yet another paradox. The paradox resides in the attempt to hold in tension the seemingly opposing forces of childhood and those of adulthood and is resolved only when we draw upon the strengths of both. In other words, it is not a question of "either-or" but one of "both-and", embracing and celebrating each phase of human becoming. Once more, the journey into the mystery of the Divine leads us into the place where children play before the face of the God who invites us to recapture some of our innocence and delight while, at the same time, recognising and accepting our responsibility to act as mature adults. We are able to do this, not by any virtue of our own, but solely through the gifting of God, the gift of enlightenment, the gift of Wisdom, which is under the gaze of God, the source of all enlightenment, not only the source of our enlightenment but also the fruit of enlightenment.

Wisdom is the gift for which the Church prays on December 17 each year in one of the Advent O antiphons: "O Wisdom coming forth from the mouth of the Most High, reaching from one end to the other, mightily and sweetly ordering all things. Come and teach us the way of prudence."

Before all that is came into being, Wisdom was the outpouring of God's eternal love. "The Lord created me at the beginning of his work, the first of his acts of old ... before the beginning of the earth ... then I was beside him, like a master workman, and I was daily his delight, rejoicing before him always, rejoicing in his inhabited world and delighting in the sons of men" (Prov. 8: 22-31). Wisdom is the delight in the eye of God Who beholds us and gives Himself to us at each and every phase of the journey into life. "Wisdom is radiant and unfading and she is easily discerned by those who love her, and is found by those who seek her. She hastens to make herself known to those who desire her ... because she goes about seeking those worthy of her, and she graciously appears to them in their paths and meets them in every thought" (Wis. 6: 12-16).

It was along a path in Galilee that Wisdom encountered and captivated Andrew and his companion. The Baptist points to Jesus and calls him the Lamb of God, whereupon Andrew and the other disciple, consumed by curiosity, follow him. "Jesus turned and saw them following, and said to them, 'What do you seek?' And they said to him, 'Rabbi, where are you staying?' He said to them, 'Come and see.' They came and saw where he was staying, and they stayed with him that day" (Jn.1: 37 -39). It was along the road to Emmaus that we find a similar type of encounter: casual, unexpected, enriching, life changing. Two disciples, sorrowing over the death of Jesus, confused and distressed, encounter the gift of Wisdom, who rebukes them for being foolish and then feeds and comforts them, a Wisdom which so fires their souls that they immediately return to Jerusalem. The encounter takes place on the road, not in the Temple or synagogue, but in the hustle and bustle of everyday life. Such is the way in which the Wisdom of God communicates herself.

Wisdom is the gift which informs the response of the human heart under the gaze of God. One response to the gift of Wisdom is the form of prayer we call *Lectio Divina*. Lectio Divina is much wider than simply reading a spiritual book and reflecting on its contents; it involves adopting a listening stance before God, alert to the in-breaking of God as and when He pleases to reveal Himself. Lectio Divina is the finding of God in all that is, the beauty of a sunset; the smile of a friend; the senselessness of gratuitous violence; the emaciated body of a child who is starving; the song of the wind dancing in the trees; nothing, but nothing, is excluded from the gaze of God. All things come together to those who love God, yes, as St Augustine reminds us, even our sins, for it is through Wisdom that we respond, as Mary did, with a profound *fiat*, knowing that all will be well.

Faithfulness to daily prayer brings with it the reward of a wisdom which allows us to discern the presence and activity of God in the daily events which befall us. Wisdom is the inner sense which gives us a "feel for God." It brings with it a thirst or a curiosity to know more of God. Wisdom resides in that insight and discernment which allows us to be surprised, startled, and awe-struck when it touches the depths of our being. Wisdom lies at the heart of Ignatius of Loyola's fourteen rules on discernment. According to him, we become enlightened through being sensitised to the origins of those movements which prompt us to grow in holiness. In the context of the *Spiritual Exercises*, Ignatius encourages us to reflect upon these movements and learn from them. For the second week of the Exercises, he proposes a further set of eight rules for a deeper discernment of spirits in order to help us become yet more sensitive to the wellspring of human motivation. The focus is primarily, but not exclusively, upon inner movements and the way they affect the way we think, feel, and act. That discernment, which is the work of Wisdom, is not restricted to the time of retreat, but, like the air we breathe, permeates our lives and presents us with a challenge to see the hand of God at work in every waking moment of our existence.

The past five chapters have taken us on a journey, first of all, into that special place of infancy where the overriding image is that of the reciprocal gaze of mother and infant at the breast, a gaze which reflects the intimacy of the gaze of God. We are brought into being by the gaze of our mother, but more profoundly, we are brought into life by the creative gaze of God. There we faced the first crisis of human development, namely, the resolution of the conflict between trust and mistrust. Then we moved into the place where hope is the central focus. Drawing on the insight of the prophetic experience, hope in God was seen, at least in one of its manifestations, as the instrument for the resolution of conflict. The third chapter focused upon the perpetual movement of conversion, a movement into which we are drawn by the constant gaze of God. Here we looked at spiritual development as a series of movements which mirror human growth, where spiritual development calls for movement away from rigidity to flexibility; from self-rejection towards self-acceptance; from dependence towards autonomy; from need towards desire; from selfishness towards altruism. In the fourth chapter, the journey we took was into the barren tracts of the wilderness, a place which both calls us to freedom and confronts us with the desolate experiences we are exposed to as human beings. In the present chapter, we traced the cyclical patterns of the seasons of the soul, linking the four blessings with which the gaze of God enriches the human spirit: the movement from the winter blessing of cleansing to spring with its blessing of making beautiful; to summer with its blessing of enriching; and, finally, to the fruitfulness of autumn with its blessing of enlightenment. The dance goes on and will go on forever into eternity, where we continue to blossom under the tender gaze of God.

The journeys we have taken have rarely been easy. Much of the time, they were difficult and demanding. We may draw comfort from the fact that most classical journeys were arduous. Mircea Eliade, in his essay *The Myth of the Eternal Return or Cosmos and History,* reminds us that the quest upon which Jason and the Argonauts set out was hazardous and life threatening. Odysseus embarked on his quest to return home and faced many dangers in Homer's *Odyssey*. Virgil's *Aeneid* is equally a tale of the life-changing journey taken by Aeneas from Troy. The personal quest to which Eliade draws our attention is the quest to find the centre of the self, We understand that features of the journey are replicated in our journey into union with God. "The road is arduous, fraught with perils, because it is, in fact, a rite of passage from the profane to the sacred, from the ephemeral and illusory to reality and eternity, from death to life, from man to divinity."[20] The journey "from the ephemeral and illusory to reality and eternity" is the overarching journey in this book, a journey which encapsulates and underpins all those other journeys. This particular journey demonstrates why I have insisted that spiritual development engages us in a cyclical movement. It is the journey from time to eternity, a journey which allows God to rectify the mistakes of the past and redeem our tomorrows. If, as Eliot conjectures, time lies eternally in the

---

[20] M. Eliade, *The Myth of the Eternal Return or, Cosmos and History,* Translated from the French by Willard R Trask, (Princeton University Press, 1974) 18.

present moment, then it is irredeemable, as I mentioned at the beginning of the book. Spiritual growth involves allowing the God of our tomorrows to bring us out of the present moment, in fact, to bring us out of the temporal dimension altogether. Encounter with God in prayer draws us into the realm of the eternal because He dwells outside time, and when we allow Him into our hearts, then that encounter must lie outside time. What this accomplishes, as we spend time with God in prayer, is that our past, present, and future lie open to the gaze of God. As a consequence, the Lord is able to touch our yesterdays with His healing gaze. This means that the failings of the past, as I have mentioned before, the regrets we have over mistakes made, regrets over words we wish we hadn't said, are healed by the touch of the Divine Physician. This is why it is essential to understand spiritual growth and development as one transcending time and allowing us to return, in Eliot's words, to the place where we started and discover the place for the first time. We discover the place for the first time because we see a place renewed, cleaned, healed, and enlightened by the gaze of God, a living gaze which has mended the mistakes of the past and healed the wounds of time.

I end this chapter, and with it the book, with the prayer taken from Ephesians: My prayer for you is "that the Father of Glory may give you a spirit of wisdom and of revelation in the knowledge of him, having the eyes of your hearts enlightened, that you may know what is the hope to which he has called you." (Eph.1:17-18). My prayer is that you may more readily discern how the wisdom of God becomes effective in the weakness and foolishness of the human heart, for as Paul reminds us, "the foolishness of God is wiser than men and the weakness of God is stronger than men" (1 Cor. 1:25).

Holding fast to this truth will enlighten the eyes of your hearts and enable you to see more clearly the hope to which we are called. In his book *The Little Prince,* Antoine de Saint Exupery goes to the heart of how to read the signs illuminated by the wondrous gaze of God. What better way, therefore, is there for me to say good-bye than by citing the words with which the fox made his farewell to the Little Prince? "Good-bye," said the fox. "Here is my secret. It's quite simple. One sees clearly only with the heart. Anything essential is invisible to the eyes."[21]

---

[21] A. De Saint Exupery, *The Little Prince,* Ttranslated from the French by Richard Howard, (Egmont UK Limited, in association with Harcourt, Inc., 2005) 63.

References

Biblical quotations, unless otherwise stated, are taken from the Revised Standard Version of the Bible, edited by Herbert G. May and Bruce M Metzger, Revised1946-1952. Second Edition of the New Testament 1971.

Alcock, J. E. "Religion and Rationality." In *Religion and Mental Health,* Ed. John F. Schumaker, Oxford University Press, 1992.

Augustine of Hippo *Confessions*, VII, xvii, 23.

Bacon, F. *Essays, Civil and Moral. Vol. III, Part 1. The Harvard Classics.* New York: F. Collier & Son, 1909–14; Bartleby.com, 2001. www.bartleby.com/3/1/. accessed 11/04/2014.

Bell, R. M. *Holy Anorexics.* Chicago University Press, 1985.

Berger, P. L. and T. Luckmann *The Social Construction of Reality,* Harmondsworth: Penguin Books, 1971.

Boswell, J. *The Life of Samuel Johnson*, LLD, Vol. III.

Bright, J. *A History of Israel.* Second Edition, London: SCM Press, 1972.

Brown, R. E. *The Birth of the Messiah.* London: Geoffrey Chapman, 1977.

Bultmann, R. *Jesus and the Word,* Translated by L.P. Smith and E.H. Lantero, Fontana, 1958.

Bulrmann, R. *"The Early Christian Concept of Hope"* in *Theological Dictionary of the New Testament,* vol. II, ed. Gerhard Kittel, Trans. Geoffrey W. Bromley, Grand Rapids, Michigan: Wm. B. Eerdmans, 1964.

Brown, R. E. *The Birth of the Messiah,* London: Geoffrey Chapman 1977.

Cassian, J. *The Twelve Books of John Cassian on the Institutes of the Coeobia and the Remedies for the Eight Principal Faults*, trans. Rev Edgar C.S. Gibson, M.A., 2012, Veritas Splendor Publications (Kindle edition).

Cox, M. *Mysticism: The Direct Experience of God.* The Aquarian Press, 1983.

de Saint Exupery, A., *The Little Prince,* Translated from the French by Richard Howard, Egmont UK Limited in association with Harcourt Inc. 2005.

Donne, J. "The Bell, Devotions upon Emergent Occasions," in *The Oxford Book of English Prose,* chosen and edited by Sir Arthur Quiller-Couch (Clarendon Press, Oxford, 1973).

Eckhart, Meister, *The Essential Sermons, Commentaries, Treatises, and Defence,* Translation and Introduction by Edmund Colledge, O.S.A. and Bernard McGinn, *The Classics of Western Spirituality.* London: SPCK, 1981.

Eliade, M. *The Myth of the Eternal Return, or Cosmos and History.* Translated from the French by Willard R Trask Princeton University Press, 1974.

Eliot, T.S. "East Coker,", In *Four Quartets*. Revised Edition, Faber & Faber, 1979.

Erikson, E.H. *Identity Youth and Crisis*. New York and London: W. W. Norton & Co, 1968.

Erikson, E. H., J.M. Erikson, and H.Q. Kivnick, *Vital Involvement in Old Age*. New York and London: W. W. Norton & Co, 1989.

Erikson, E. In Lewis and Volkmar, *Clinical Aspects of Child and Adolescent Development*. Third Edition, Lea and Febiger, 1990.

Franklin, B. *Poor Richard's Almanack,* June 1758, The Complete Poor Richard Almanacks, facsimile ed., vol. 2.

Freud, S. "Beyond the Pleasure Principle," in *Abstracts of the Standard Edition of the Complete Works of Sigmund Freud*, edited by Carrie Lee Rothgeb, Jason Aaronson, 1987.

Fleming, D. SJ. *The Spiritual Exercises of St Ignatius*. St Louis: The Institute of Jesuit Resources, 1978, Second Printing, 1980.

Frey-Rohn, H. "Evil from the Psychological Point of View," In *Evil*: *Curatorium of the C.G. Jung Institute of Zurich*. Evanston, Ill.: Northwestern University Press, 1967.

Gibran, K. *The Prophet*. Originally published in 1923 by Alfred A. Knopf. Kindle edition.

Greenacre, P. "The Childhood of the Artist: Libidinal Phase Development and Giftedness," in *The Psychoanalytic Study of the Child,* Vol. 12. New York: International Universities Press, 1957.

Gribomont, J. "Eastern Christianity," in *Christian Spirituality: Origins to the Twelfth Century* Edited by Bernard McGinn and John Meyendorff, Vol. 16 of *World Spirituality: An Encyclopedic History of the Religious Quest,* New York, Crossroads.

Grippando, J. *"L'espoir c'est le dernier à mourir,"* translated by Corinne Rouach, State Museum of Auschwitz-Birkenau, Oświęcim, 2008.

Guigo II. *The Ladder of Monks and Twelve Meditations,* translated by Edmund College O.S.A and James Walsh S.J. Mowbray, 1978.

Gutierrez, G. *A Theology of Liberation,* SCM Press, 1981.

Hammerskjold, D. *Markings,* Translated from the Swedish by Leif Sjöberg. W. H. Auden, London, 1966.

Hillesum, E. *An Interrupted Life: The Diaries of Etty Hillesum, 1941-43,* New York, London: Washington Square Press, 1985.

Hilton, W. *The Scale of Perfection.* Scanned and edited by Harry Plantinga. This e-text is in the public domain, Chapter XIV, First Book, Part 1.

Huxley, A. *The Perennial Philosophy* New York, London: Harper Perennial Modern Classics, 2009.

Ignatius of Loyola. *Exercitia Spiritualis,* Rome, Monumenta Historica Societatis Jesu, 1969.

Jeeves, M., and W.S. Brown, *Neuroscience Psychology and Religion: Illusions, Delusions, and Realities about Human Nature.* West Conshohocken, Pennsylvania: Templeton Foundation Press 2009.

John of the Cross. *Spiritual Canticle, The Complete Works of St. John of the Cross, vols. I, II, III,* Translated and Edited by E Allison Peers. Westminster, Maryland: The Newman Press, 1953 (revised edition).

Jones, A. *Exploring Spiritual Direction.* Seabury Press, 1999.

Jung, C. G. *Psychology and Religion: West and East.* Princeton University Press in the U.S. and Routledge & Kegan Paul in the U.K. Chapter V, "Psychotherapy for the Clergy,"§ 519-520.

Kant, I. *Der Streit der Fakultäten,* in *Gesammelte Schriften,* vol. 7, 1917.

Keats, J. "Ode to Autumn," in *The Oxford Book of English Verse, 1250-1918,* chosen and edited by Sir Arthur Quiller Couch, Second Edition, Second Edition, Oxford University Press, 1987.

Kegan, R. *The Evolving Self: Problem and Process in Human Development.* Cambridge, Massachusetts, and London: Harvard University Press, 1982.

Knowles, M. S. *The Modern Practice of Adult Education.* Association Press, New York, 1970.

Kohut, H. *The Restoration of the Self.* International Universities Press, 1977.

Landinsky, D. *Love Poems from God.* Penguin Putnam Group, 2002.

Lawrence, D. H. *The Hands of the Living God. The Complete Poems.* Edited by Vivian de Sola Pinto and Warren Roberts. Harmondsworth, Middlesex: Penguin Books, 1991.

Matthew, I. *The Impact of God*. Hodder and Stoughton, 1995.

May, G. *Care of Mind, Care of Spirit,* San Francisco:Harper and Row, 1982.

May, G. *The Dark Night of the Soul*: *A Psychiatrist Explores the Connection Between Darkness and Spiritual Growth* (e-book edition), 2004.

McFague, S. *Models of God: Theology for an Ecological, Nuclear Age*. Philadelphia: Fortress Press, 1987.

McGinn et al. "The Uplifting Spirituality of Pseudo-Dionysius," In *Christian Spirituality: Origins to the Twelfth Century* vol. 16, *World Spirituality: An Encyclopaedic History of the Religious Quest*. New York: Crossroad, 1985.

McKenzie, J. L., SJ. "The Gospel According to Matthew, "in, *The Jerome Biblical Commentary*, Edited by Raymond F Brown, SS, Joseph A. Fitzmyer, SJ, and Roland F Murphy, O. Carm. London: Geoffrey Chapman,1969.

McQuarrie, J. *Christian Hope*. S.C.M. Press Ltd., 1978.

Meissner, W. W. *Primacy of Spiritual Experience in Theological Reflection*. Boston: Lonergan Workshop Journal, vol. IV.

Milner, M. *The Suppressed Madness of Sane Men*. Routledge, London and New York: 1987.

Moltmann, J. *Theology of Hope*. London and New York: SCM Press, 1967.

Morton, H. V. *A Stranger in Spain*. London: Methuen, paperback edition, 1983.

Mother Teresa *Mother Teresa: Come Be My Light*. Edited with commentary by Brian Kolodiejchuk, London, Boston, Sydney, Auckland:: Rider, Kindle edition.

Newburg, A., et al. *Why God Won't Go Away: Brain Science and the Biology of Belief.* New York: Ballantine Books, 2002.

Pannenberg, W. *Jesus, God, and Man*. Translated by Lewis L. Wilkins and Duane A. Priebe London: SCM Press, 1968.

Pearse, P. H. *The Fool*. Electronic edition compiled by Pádraig Bambury, CELT: Corpus of Electronic Texts: a project of University College, Cork, www.ucc.ie/celt, 1998,

Rawson, H., and M. Milne (ed.). *The Oxford Dictionary of American Quotations,* Oxford: Oxford University Press, 2006.

Rizzuto, A. M. "Religious Development: A Psychoanalytic Point of View," *New Directions for Child Development,* 52, Jossey-Bass. Summer 1992.

Rorem, P. "The Uplifting Spirituality of Pseudo-Dionysius," In McGinn et al., *Christian Spirituality. Origins to the Twelfth Century* vol. 16, *World Spirituality: An Encyclopedic History of the Religious Quest* New York: Crossroad, 1985.

Rorem. P. In *Pseudo-Dionysius: The Complete Works*. The Classics of Western Spirituality. New York: Paulist Press, 1987.

Rudnytsky, P. *The Psychoanalytic Vocation: Rank, Winnicott and the Legacy of Freud.* New Haven: Yale University Press. 1991.

Salkind, N. J. *Theories of Human Development*. New York: John Wiley and Sons, 1985.

Schillebeeckx, E. *God, the Future of Man*. London and Sydney: T & T Clark, 1969.

Shaffer, P. *Equus* Athenium Press, 1973.

Silverman, D. "Attachment Research: An Approach to a Developmental Relational Perspective," In *Relational Perspectives in Psychoanalysis,* Eds. Skolnick, N.J. Warshaw, S.C. Hillsdale, N.J: The Analytic Press, 1992.

Spitz, R. A. *The First Year of Life: A Psychoanalytic Study of Normal and Deviant Development of Object Relations.* New York: International Universities Press, 1965.

Suchocki, M. H. *The End of Evil: Process Eschatology in Historical Context.* Albany: State University of New York Press, 1988.

Swimme, B. *The Universe Is a Green Dragon,* Rochester VT: Bear and Co., 2001.

Tauler, J. *The Inner Way*. Translated by Arthur Wollaston Hutton, London: Methuen and Co. 1901.

Teilhard de Chardin, P. *Le Milieu Divin.* New York: Collins, Fontana Books, 1978.

Teresa of Avila *The Life of St Teresa of Jesus*, Translated by David Lewis, fifth edition, London: Thomas Baker, 1932.

Teresa of Avila From *Hispanic Anthology: Poems Translated from the Spanish by English and North American Poets*. Collected and arranged by Thomas Walsh, New York: G. P. Putnam's Sons, 1920.

Teresa of Avila "When the Holy Thaws," In D. Landinsky, *Love Poems from God*. Penguin Putnam Group, 2002.

The Cloud of Unknowing. Harmondsworth, Middlesex: Penguin Books, Ltd. 1981.

The Poetry of Thomas Hood (Kindle edition), Portable Poetry, 2013.

Toner, J., S.J. *A Commentary on Saint Ignatius' Rules for the Discernment of Spirits: A Guide in the Principles and Practice*. St Louis: The Institute of Jesuit Sources, 1982.

Underhill, E. *Mystics of the Church* Cambridge: James Clarke, 1925.

Vaillant, G. E. *Adaptation to Life*. Boston, Toronto: Little, Brown and Co. 1977.

Wiesel, E. *Night*, 1969, cited in Moltmann, J. *The Crucified God*. London: Harper and Row, second edition, 1973.

Wilde, O. *The Ballad of Reading Gaol*. Wordsworth Editions Ltd. 1898.

Winnicott, D. W. *The Child, the Family and the Outside World*. London: Penguin, 1964.

Winnicott, D. W. "Morals and Education" In *The Maturational Processes and the Facilitating Environment*. Madison, CT International Universities Press, 1965.

Winnicott, D. W. *Human Nature.* New York: Scholoken Books, 1988.

Winnicott, D. W. *Through Paediatrics to Psycho-Analysis, Collected Papers,* New York: Brunner/Mazel 1992.

Wulff, D. M. *Psychology of Religion: Classical and Contemporary* (2nd Edition). New York: John Wiley and Sons, 1997.

Lightning Source UK Ltd.
Milton Keynes UK
UKHW011848170822
407466UK00008B/423/J

9 781664 113459